Legal Aspects of Midwifery Workbook

FOR PRACTITIONERS AND STUDENTS OF MIDWIFERY

Bridgit Dimond
MA, LLB, DSA, AHSM, ACIA, Barrister
Emeritus Professor of the University of Glamorgan

Dorothy Walters
RGN, RM, ADM, Cert Ed (FE)

Books for Midwives Press
An imprint of Hochland & Hochland Ltd

Dedicated to Ruth Davies in acknowledgement of her immense contribution to the profession and practice of midwifery

Published by Books for Midwives Press, 174a Ashley Road, Hale, Cheshire, WA15 9SF, England

© Dimond and Walters, 1997

First edition

All rights reserved. No part of this book may be reproduced in any form or by any electronic or mechanical means, including information storage and retrieval systems, without permission in writing from the publisher, except by a reviewer who may quote passages in a review.

ISBN 1-898507-43-0

British Library Cataloguing in Publication Data
A catalogue record for this book is available from the British Library

Printed in Great Britain by Cromwell Press Ltd

Contents

Acknowledgements — *v*
Introduction — *vi*
Assessment strategy — *xi*

Section One
The Legal System — 1

Section Two
Professional Accountability — 14

Section Three
Client Centred Care, Consent to Treatment and Information Giving — 22

Section Four
Records, Confidentiality and Access — 29

Section Five
Civil Liability: Negligence — 36

Section Six
Employment Law — 42

Section Seven
Health and Safety Law — 49

Section Eight
The Midwife Working in the Community and Midwife Managed Units — 64

Section Nine
The Legal Aspects of Medication — 75

Section Ten
Specific Areas of Law — 81

Bibliography — *94*

Appendices

One:	Personal reflections and planned learning activities record	95
Two:	Format for reporting cases of alleged misconduct by practising midwives to the LSA	96
Three:	Format for systematic evaluation of a significant incident or professional issue	99
Four:	Self review form for practising midwives	103
Five:	Complaints about professional conduct	106

Offprints

I:	Complementary therapy and the midwife	109
II:	Local pay guidance for purchasers	114
III:	Midwifery-managed units	116
IV:	Medication and the midwife: statutory control	121
V:	The midwife's power to prescribe	125
VI:	In vitro fertilization and the law	128
VII:	The scope of fertility treatment	133

Index   *135*

Acknowledgements

The authors thank all those midwives who give so readily of their time in the course of duty and meet the challenges of late twentieth century maternity care and to whom this workbook is also dedicated.

In particular the contributions of three midwives, Sian Anderson, Tanneke Berwick and Geraldine Protheroe are acknowledged for their time and effort exerted in piloting the exercises. The critical readers for the workbook were Professor R. Bryar of the School of Community Health Care, Hull University and Ms Louise Silverton Director of Education and Professional Development, RCM, London. Their considered, constructive comments have been valued in the development of this workbook. Kate Harmond is thanked for her permission to reproduce Appendix 2. The UKCC and publishers of Modern Midwife are acknowledged for their permission to reproduce extracts in the appendices.

Colleagues in the University of Glamorgan are thanked for their support and encouragement.

Finally, a big thank you to our families for their patience and support.

Introduction

Midwives cannot ignore the fact that their work takes place within the context of the law. You need to have an understanding of the law relating to the rights of the mother and child, and your own professional duties, some of which are set out in the Midwives Rules (UKCC, 1993).

The broad aim of this workbook

The workbook is designed to help you to further develop knowledge and understanding of the legal system and those areas of the law which affect the practice of midwifery.

There are also opportunities for assessment of academic ability.

You are the best person to identify your own continuing education needs and at what level you would like to be assessed.

You can self identify learning outcomes that are evidence based and relate this to your own practice environment.

Pathways to academic credit

You can choose the route which suits your professional needs:

You determine your entry point. This is your workbook - make it work for you.

Option One

Use your workbook as a **DISTANCE LEARNING MODULE** within an approved Level 3 programme.

Option Two

Use the **IDENTIFIED COMPONENTS** within the workbook which will give you the opportunity to demonstrate your ability to apply theoretical and legal principles to your practice.

These exercises can be assessed at **LEVEL 3**.

You will need to have sought advice from an appropriate APEL assessor who will provide you with the necessary criteria for success.

Option Three

Photocopy the form (Appendix 1). Once you have completed the exercises, fill the form in and put it into your **PERSONAL PROFESSIONAL PROFILE.**

This can then be used to provide evidence of your continuing professional development.

How to use the workbook

This workbook has been designed to be read in parallel with the textbook, *The Legal Aspects of Midwifery* by Bridgit Dimond (referred to as 'the Textbook'). Each section of the unit is linked with specific chapter(s) of the textbook and it is recommended that the relevant chapter(s) should be read before the section is begun. Other references should be easily followed up and will be listed at the end of each section. Not all the law relevant to midwives can be covered, and the opportunity is there for further study of other topics. The section on specialist topics gives you a choice of issues to be covered but if you find yourself with additional time you can cover more than the required number of options.

Activities suggested within each section

At specific stages of each section, you will see symbols suggesting you undertake an activity. This is designed to enhance understanding of the textbook and to apply the theory to a practical task. You have the opportunity to apply the law to particular situations and to reflect on the issues raised and self-assess your understanding of the legal principles.

The activities in the *Legal Aspects of Midwifery Workbook* are designed to help you develop as an active learner.

The *Legal Aspects of Midwifery Workbook* could be validated and give credit towards a diploma or first degree.

Throughout the workbook activities, you will be asked to relate your learning to your practice.

The following symbols are used to identify different types of activity.

This symbol directs your attention to essential reading in the main text book *The Legal Aspects of Midwifery* or to other identified sources.

This symbol draws your attention to a useful offprint provided to assist your study.

This symbol denotes an activity which requires you to list, explain, or provide evidence of your level of knowledge and how you have applied this to your professional practice.

This symbol denotes an activity which requires you to discuss options with colleagues, explore alternative views and share the outcome of the activity with your colleagues and supervisor.

Whenever you see this symbol you should reflect upon previous knowledge or professional practice. This should enable you to relate the activity to current practice.

The clock symbol provides you with a guide to the time required to complete the activities. The pace of work will vary, depending on your personal circumstances and needs.

This symbol denotes activities within the workbook which can be developed as evidence of your ability to identify, analyse, justify and substantiate your conclusions. Any one, or all of these activities can be assessed.

By using the activities in the workbook you will be able to work at your own pace, stage your progress through the activities and seek academic credit for certain activities within the workbook.

You are in control of the pace and depth of learning.

Introduction

Some of the activities require you to obtain circulars and other information from your employer, local supervising authority or other sources. This material is listed in the bibliography so that you can start obtaining it now so that you will not be held up when you come to do the activity. It is assumed that all students have copies of the United Kingdom Central Council for Nursing, Midwifery and Health Visiting publications. If not the UKCC should be contacted to obtain the documents. In addition midwives should read articles in the many journals now available which supplement the topics covered in this workbook.

List of UKCC documentation (essential reading):

1. Midwives Rules (1993)
2. The Midwife's Code of Practice (1994)
3. Code of Professional Conduct for the Nurse, Midwife and Health Visitor (1992)
4. The Scope of Professional Practice (1992)
5. A Guide for Students of Nursing and Midwifery (1992)
6. Standards for the Administration of Medicines (1992)
7. Standards for Records and Record Keeping (1993)
8. UKCC Guidelines for Professional Practice (1996)
9. UKCC Position statement on clinical supervision for nursing and health visiting (April, 1996)
10. UKCC Reporting misconduct - information for employers and managers (August, 1996)
11. UKCC Reporting unfitness to practise - information for employers and managers (August, 1996).

The above documents are published by the United Kingdom Central Council for Nurses, Midwives and Health Visitors and can be obtained from:

UKCC, 23 Portland Place, London W1N 3AF.

Note you are encouraged to reflect upon the content and practical application of each section in the workbook.

You can prepare and record evidence of your learning activities from each section. This record is then suitable for inclusion in your personal professional profile.

You can choose your own format for use in your Personal Professional Profile, or use the form provided in Appendix 1 (this can be photocopied as often as you require).

On completion of this workbook you should:

1. Be able to understand the legal significance of most situations likely to be encountered.
2. Understand how the law protects and defines the rights of the client.
3. Know at what point it is necessary to bring in the professional lawyer.
4. Write protocols within the legal framework.
5. Be able to further examine the legislative framework surrounding midwifery practice.
6. Be able to provide evidence of your ability to evaluate practices from a legal perspective.
7. When appropriate, provide evidence of your ability to promote changes in practice to safeguard the public and fellow practitioners.

Suggested action on completion of this workbook

Once you have completed your workbook and personal records, seek opportunities to share and discuss the outcomes with your preceptor, your supervisor of midwives and especially your colleagues.

This workbook provides you with a unique opportunity to learn, as you explore legal issues confronting midwives every day.

Assessment Strategy

This workbook provides the midwifery practitioner with a variety of opportunities to gain academic credit for the completion of selected activities.

The level of study and achievement of the expected learning outcomes will be determined by *you*.

The components of study for assessment at Level 3 are clearly identified in the following sections.

Professional accountability
Page 17, Midwives and Supervision.

You are required to:

a) Study the duties of the Supervisor of Midwives and the responsibilities of the midwife as outlined in the Rules and the Codes of Professional Practice and Midwife's Code of Practice. Review the current literature relating to midwifery and clinical supervision.
b) Undertake a SWOT analysis of the relationship which exists between yourself and your supervisor.
c) In the light of this SWOT analysis, draw up an action plan to make this relationship more effective.
d) Present your findings to your supervisor and discuss any recommended changes.

If you are a supervisor of midwives, undertake this exercise in relation to the midwives you supervise.

Keep a record of this exercise and the outcomes for your Personal Professional Profile.

Health and safety law
Page 72, Assessment opportunity (suitable for assessment at level 3).

a) Using the principles of Risk Management, prepare a checklist for midwives which will enable them to identify those issues and potential dangers to personal and clients safety.
b) Evaluate the responses to the checklist and develop protocols to reduce risk to clients and staff.

c) Prepare a programme of training and education for colleagues and other staff related to the locally identified needs.

Keep a record of this exercise and the outcomes for your Personal Professional Profile.

There are other opportunities for assessment. *You* are the best person to identify your own continuing education needs and at what level you would like to be assessed.

You can self identify learning outcomes that are evidence based and relate this to your own practice environment.

This is your workbook – make it work for you.

SECTION ONE

The Legal System

On completion of this section you should be able to:

- Define the main sources of the law.

- Name the statute which enables the nurse, midwife and health visitor to practice.

- Understand the difference in the proceedings in civil and criminal courts.

- Develop an understanding of legal terminology.

Within this section is an assessment opportunity. This could be suitable for accreditation for prior learning (APL) assessment.

Alternatively this assessment may be used as the summative assessment for a distance learning module.

SECTION ONE

The Legal System

It is essential that the midwife has an understanding of how the legal system works, what gives legal effect to a principle or declaration so that it becomes a law, what procedure is followed, what are the functions of the different courts and what do some of the terms used by lawyers mean. This first section is designed to introduce the midwife to this field.

This section covers the following areas:

- The sources of law: European community law, statute law and the common law and categories of law
- Midwives Rules and UKCC Codes and the difference in law between them
- The different courts and their function
- The legal personnel: the lawyers which are divided between barristers and solicitors, the judges
- The procedure
- The language
- The distinction between law and ethics.

The sources of law

Law derives from two main sources (see p. xiv of the textbook):

- Act of Parliament (known as statute law)
- judge made law (known as the common law).

Acts of Parliament take supremacy over all other laws apart from those made by the European Community, because as a result of this country signing the Treaty of Rome, this country is now bound by the laws made by the European Community.

An Act of Parliament must be passed through the two Houses of Parliament and then signed by the Queen before it becomes law. It may come into force the day it is signed or a later date (or dates) may be given for different sections or the whole act to come into force. Sections of some acts are still not in force many years after they were passed (for example, there are several sections of the Disabled Persons [Services, Consultation, and Representation] Act 1986 which are still not in force).

Sometimes the Act of Parliament gives power to a Minister of State or another specified person or body to draw up statutory instruments covering detailed points. These would be placed before the Houses of Parliament for approval before they come into force. The textbook cites the example of the power given under section 22 of the Nurses, Midwives and Health Visitors Act 1979 to the UKCC to make rules. Rules made under section 12 (removal from and restoration to the register) cannot come into force until approved by order of the Lord Chancellor (for England and Wales) or the Lord Advocate (for Scotland). An example pertaining to midwifery practice are those mentioned on pp. 3–5 of the Midwives Rules (UKCC, 1993).

European laws

Since the acceptance by this country of the Treaty of Rome and membership of the European Community, the laws, regulations and directives of the European Community must be adhered to. A regulation of the European Community is automatically binding upon the member states without further legislation, it is known as mandatory. A directive in contrast requires the member states to enact regulations or other laws for the directive to be implemented. Thus it will be seen that the directives issued in 1992 on Health and Safety led to regulations being introduced in England and Wales which came into force on 1 January 1993 (see Section 7 on health and safety).

Interpretation of statutes and statutory instruments

There are rules relating to the interpretation of statutes and statutory instruments to ensure some consistency in their implementation. Sometimes there may be uncertainty over the interpretation and this could lead to a case being heard in the courts when the judge or judges may have to rule on how the specific section or subsection should be interpreted.

Activity | **10 minutes**

Refer to your own copy of the Midwives Rules (UKCC, 1993) and take any significant paragraph and examine critically whether its meaning is clear or whether different interpretations could be placed upon it. Get a colleague to undertake the same activity and identify if there are any areas of uncertainty in your interpretation.

Commentary

This was hopefully a difficult exercise because the Rules should be drafted in such a way that ambiguity or uncertainty over its meaning is avoided. It would therefore have been very difficult to find ambiguities.

Note that regulations or rules are mandatory i.e. they must be observed. In contrast, a code suggests that you usually should or ought to comply, but there is room for professional discretion.

Legal Aspects of Midwifery Workbook

The common law (see p. xiv)

Judges hear cases where disputes arise between individuals or institutions or where a prosecution is brought in the criminal courts. These disputes may centre on the uncertainty in the interpretation of an Act of Parliament or statutory instrument. Or they may be concerned with an area where there are no statutory provisions but the situation is governed by the common law.

Activity   1 hour

As an example of problems in statutory interpretation and relating back to the previous activity, take Rule 39 (set out in Table 2.4 on p. 18 of the textbook), the duty of the midwife to undergo medical examination.

In what circumstances could this be ordered?

- Could the employer agree with the local supervising authority (LSA) that all newly employed midwives receive a test for AIDS/HIV infection?
- Could each midwife be compelled to have routine testing for hepatitis B and C?
- What happens if the midwife refuses? Is she liable to be automatically suspended from practice by the LSA?
- How could she challenge the suspension from practice by the LSA?
- What criteria are the courts likely to use over the implications and implementation of Rule 39?
- Can the midwife continue to practice in another LSA area if she has been suspended from practice in one geographical area in which she has notified her intention to practice?

Commentary

It should be clear from this exercise how difficult it is to draft legislation to cover all possible questions which might arise.

If a midwife were to challenge a requirement to undergo a medical examination and brought an action for judicial review of the decision of the LSA, the ruling of the judge would become a precedent for future cases on similar facts. Thus there can develop a considerable body of law on the interpretation of one section or subsection.

Judges may also have to determine what the law should be in areas where there is no precedent or statute.

Thus for many years there was no statute law which defined the duty of the occupier of land to trespassers who were injured on the land. The duty of the occupier in relation to non-trespassers, or visitors, was defined by the Occupier's Liability Act 1957. The duty of the occupier to trespassers was defined in a series of court decisions culminating with the leading case of *British Railways Board* v. *Herrington*. In 1984 the Occupier's Liability Act was passed which filled the statutory gap and laid down by

The Legal System

Act of Parliament the occupier's duty towards trespassers. Similarly the definition of the reasonable standard of care to be exercised by a professional is not set out in statute but by the common law in a case decided by a judge in 1957. From the name of the case it has been called 'The Bolam Test' and its implications are discussed in Section 5 on civil accountability and the laws of negligence.

The following questions arise about the common law:

- How is it decided which court's decision should be followed if there is a conflict in the decisions from different courts?
- Who decides what the court laid down in each case?

The first question is answered by understanding the hierarchy of courts and the system of precedence. This is covered later in the section.

The second question is answered by the system of court reports.

Court reports

The details of the cases including the facts of the dispute, the arguments put before the court and the speeches of the judges are recorded in official reports of the court, which the judge will read and agree that it forms a correct record of what took place. These reports are available in any law library. Since 1865 a Council was established to ensure that the reports were reliable and accurate. In 1870 this Council became known as the Incorporated Council of Law Reporting for England and Wales. Reporters, who must be barristers, are employed to record the facts and the judgments of the cases. Thus an authorized series of reports are published. Each has its own reference number. Other series have developed covering medical law and other specialist topics.

Activity **10 minutes**

Look up on pages ix-x of the textbook the list of cases set out and decipher the reference on the basis of the following abbreviations:

1 All ER 1993 821 = volume 1 of the All England Reports for 1993 at p. 821
AC stands for Appeals Court the House of Lords
WLR stands for weekly law reports

Additional specialist series of reports have been established such as the medical law reports:
Med LR stands for Medical Law reports

If you have access to a law library take one of the significant cases such as *Airdale NHS Trust* v. *Bland* or *Whitehouse* v. *Jordan* and see if you can find the full report of the case in the library.

5

The Midwives Rules, the Midwife's Code of Practice and the Code of Professional Conduct

It should be clear from the previous discussion that whilst the Rules are part of the law being enacted under the statutory authority given by the Nurses, Midwives and Health Visitors Act 1979, the Codes do not have the same status. They are not law in themselves, but guidance which the UKCC strongly recommends should be followed but failure to follow the guidance will not necessarily constitute unlawful or misconduct in itself. Clearly evidence of failure to observe the Codes could be used in professional misconduct proceedings, but evidence could be given as to why it was reasonable in all the circumstances of the case, for the clauses of the code not to be followed. This defence would not be available where the Rules are not followed. It is clear how important records will be to establish the reasons why the midwife acted in the way she did.

Different kinds of law

There are different ways of classifying kinds of law. One is the distinction between criminal law and civil law. The former relates to an act or omission which can be followed by criminal proceedings. Usually these are brought in the name of the crown and represent the state bringing an action against a private citizen. However it is possible for a private individual to bring a private prosecution alleging that the accused is guilty of the offence with which he is charged.

Civil relates to those proceedings between private citizens or private and public bodies in which specific harm or civil wrong is alleged. The largest category of civil wrongs are known as 'torts'. These cover such civil wrongs as: negligence, trespass, nuisance, defamation and breach of a statutory duty. Breach of contract cases are civil cases but do not come under the name of torts.

Many actions or omissions may be both criminal and civil wrongs. Thus to assault a person would be a criminal act as well as a trespass to the person, a civil wrong. The law makers can decide at any time if an act should become or cease to be regarded as a criminal wrong. Thus under the Suicide Act 1961 it ceased to be a criminal act to attempt to commit suicide. However it remains a criminal act for a person to aid, abet or in any way assist another person to commit suicide.

The different courts and their function

We discussed above the system of court hierarchies. Figure 1.1 shows the civil courts and indicates that the decisions of the House of Lords is binding on all lower courts on similar facts. Figure 1.2 illustrates the courts which deal with criminal cases. Again any decisions by the House of Lords will bind all courts below it on similar facts.

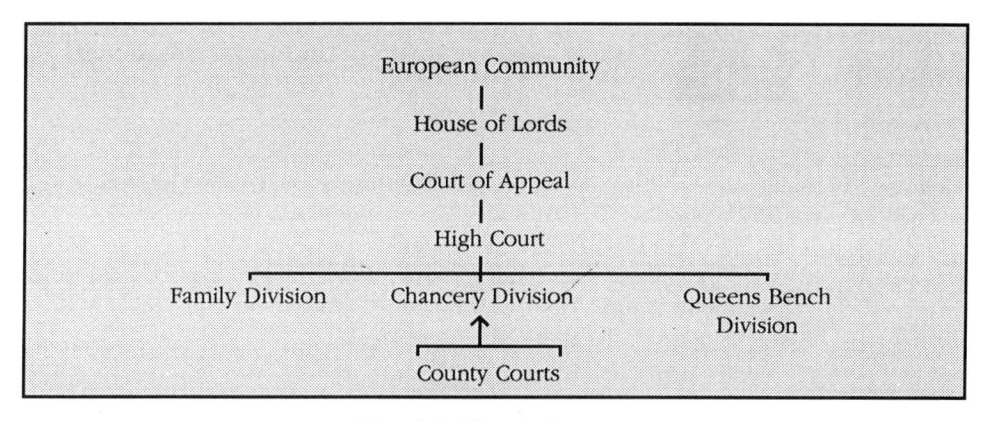

```
                    European Community
                            |
                       House of Lords
                            |
                      Court of Appeal
                            |
                        High Court
                            |
    ┌───────────────────────┼───────────────────────┐
Family Division      Chancery Division         Queens Bench
                            ↑                    Division
                    ┌───────┴───────┐
                       County Courts
```

Fig. 1.1: The civil courts

```
                       House of Lords
                            |
                      Court of Appeal
                            |
                       Crown Court
                            |
                    Magistrates Courts
```

Fig. 1.2: Criminal courts

Other courts and forums which the midwife might encounter professionally are listed below.

Coroners

The coroner holds an inquest into a death to determine the identity of the deceased, the place, time and cause of death, and the particulars required for the death to be registered (see p. 169 of the textbook for further details). This is an example of a court which is inquisitorial, not accusatorial. This means that the coroner summons the witnesses and may do most of the questioning. In contrast, a civil or criminal hearing is based on an accusatorial system, where one party is attempting to prove a case against another and the judge sits to determine the outcome with intervention only when necessary to ensure that justice is done and seen to be done.

Industrial tribunal

This forum will hear applications for unfair dismissal and other issues relating to employment. It is intended to be speedy, informal and cheap where the man in the street could present his application or defend himself. Unfortunately as employment law has become more complex, it is likely that most parties will be legally represented thus increasing the costs and further increasing the complexity of the cases.

Legal Aspects of Midwifery Workbook

Activity	**Timing for this activity will depend on you**

If you have the opportunity, visit a court hearing or industrial tribunal. All hearings are public unless the court meets in camera such as when issues relating to child care are discussed. Make yourself known to the clerk of the court and explain that you are undertaking a law course and need to understand how the legal system functions. He or she will show you where you can sit and may also be able to tell you how the case is proceeding.

Then try and answer the following questions:

- What kind of case are you listening to – civil, criminal, industrial tribunal etc?
- Who are the parties?
- Who is representing them?
- Where do they sit?
- Where do others taking part sit? Try and identify as many of the people as possible, e.g. barristers, solicitors, court clerks, court reporter, usher, the public, the witnesses, those persons involved in the case either as plaintiff or defendant or prosecutor or accused, press representatives, others?
- What sense can you make of what is happening?
- What stage has it reached? Who is giving evidence?
- Is there a jury?
- Can you distinguish between cross-examination and examination in chief? What are the differences in the type of question asked?
- How far is the judge, magistrate, coroner, chairman or other person in control intervening with questions?
- How often are other cases cited?
- How comprehensible are the proceedings to you?

Commentary
Whilst this court visit may be considered a luxury in terms of time, if any midwife is required to give evidence in court, she is strongly advised to visit the court first and familiarize herself with the surroundings, the procedure and the geography of the place. She will find that this will be extremely helpful in her preparation for giving evidence and meeting the fears of the unknown. If a midwife is required to attend any court proceedings related to work she should seek support, not only from her solicitor but a Supervisor of Midwives and/or trade union representative or friend.

The legal personnel

This consists of the lawyers, who are divided between barristers and solicitors and the judges.

There are two distinct professions for lawyers. One are the barristers, the other solicitors. They used to have more distinctive roles but gradually the distinction is weakening. They now have a common first part of training - a law degree or the successful completion of the common professional examination. Then solicitors take the Law Society's finals and study in articles with a firm of solicitors, whilst barristers take the examinations of the Council for Legal Education and become pupils in a set of chambers where barristers work on a self-employed basis. It used to be the rule that barristers took the case in court, being briefed by a solicitor to undertake the case and clients would not approach a barrister direct but only through a solicitor. However the rights of solicitors to present cases in court has gradually been extended to cover most cases and courts providing they have a recognized acceptance as a solicitor advocate.

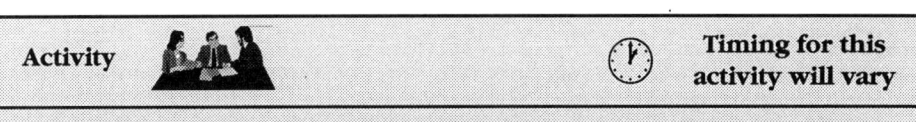

Activity	Timing for this activity will vary
Obtain from any careers department details on the training for solicitors and barristers. If possible, you may find that the solicitor employed by your trust is prepared to explain to you how cases are handled.	

The procedure

There are significant differences between the progress of a civil case and a criminal case as shown in Figure 1.3.

Criminal	Civil
A charge of a criminal offence is brought by the Crown Prosecution Service which has to show guilt beyond all reasonable doubt before a jury in the crown court or before the magistrates. In the crown court following the swearing of the jury and the plea being taken, the prosecution opens the case and its witnesses are examined in chief, cross examined and then re-examined. The Defence witnesses follow. After final speeches, the judge addresses the jury who retire to decide verdict. The judge sentences after a finding of guilty.	An alleged wrong by defendant is brought by the plaintiff who has to prove on a balance of probabilities before a judge. After the issue of a writ and its service on the defendant, documents are exchanged between the parties. At the hearing witnesses are examined in chief, cross examined and re-examined. Final speeches. Decision by judge and if appropriate enforcement of judgement.

Fig. 1.3: Procedure in civil and criminal cases compared

Legal Aspects of Midwifery Workbook

In a criminal prosecution, the burden of proof is on the prosecution to establish beyond reasonable doubt that the accused is guilty of the criminal offence with which he has been charged.

In civil proceedings, it is usually the task of the person bringing the action to prove on a balance of probabilities that the elements of the civil action which is being brought is established. As will be seen from the above, it is possible for an action to be both a civil wrong and a criminal act.

Activity 1 hour

A midwife is accused of failing to attend a mother in childbirth and it is alleged, as a result of her absence, that the mother has died. Criminal prosecution is being contemplated and in addition the family are taking legal advice to consider whether they can sue the midwife's employer for its vicarious liability for her negligence in failing to attend the mother. The substantive law on both the criminal charge and the civil action are considered in Chapters 17 and 12 respectively. Here we are concerned with the procedure in both actions.

Trace the likely course of proceedings for the criminal prosecution of the midwife and also the civil action against the employer. Identify the courts which would be involved and the legal personnel who are likely to be called upon to give advice.

Commentary

It would normally follow that if the midwife were found guilty of the criminal offence then civil liability of the employer would be admitted if she were acting in course of employment. This is because of the difference in the burden of proof.

Each midwife who has full membership of a professional organization/trade union will have additional personal indemnity for any 'samaritan acts' which she may perform off duty. The Royal College of Midwives and the Royal College of Nursing both provide personal indemnity cover for up to £3 million pounds for each such acts.

Activity 15 minutes

Now consider the following situations. These are 'events' that may be encountered and through undertaking the following activity the types of legal proceedings and possible convictions can be considered.

- A midwife is found drunk on duty. Is this unlawful?
- The same midwife has driven to her home after being suspended from duty by the line manager and Trust personnel department. Was she breaking the law by driving home?
- She failed to make adequate records in the client's clinical notes prior to being suspended from duty by her line manager. Is this unlawful?

Commentary

To be found drunk on duty would be professional misconduct and therefore actionable by the UKCC through its professional conduct committee. The midwife would also be in breech of her contract of employment and face her employer's disciplinary proceedings. She would probably not face criminal proceedings but these could follow if she drove home over the alcohol limit and therefore contrary to the Road Traffic Act. Failure to keep records would also render her liable to UKCC professional conduct proceedings and also her employers disciplinary proceedings.

The language

Midwives will have noticed that many different terms are being used which have a special legal significance. Often the law appears to be forbidding because of this unfamiliarity with the language. Every effort must be made to become familiar with some of the terms so that the language is not allowed to be a hurdle to a full understanding of the law.

> **Activity** — **Timing for this activity will vary**
>
> Turn to the Glossary in the textbook (pp. 325–28) and identify the legal terms which are used. Make out your own list of terms and as you come across terms with which you are not familiar add them to the list, looking them up in a dictionary if necessary.
>
> Test yourself at intervals to see what you can remember. Keep the score so that you can repeat the test at the end of this unit.

Commentary

You cannot expect to remember and understand the terms all at once but as you proceed through the sections of this unit, they will become more familiar to you and you will find that one of the barriers to an understanding of the law will disappear.

The distinction between law and ethics

One of the most perplexing issues for the practitioner is the distinction between law and ethics and where one begins and one ends and where does the practitioner stand if she holds ethical views which are contrary to the law.

The law as we have seen from the first section is based on the statute law or common law. Ideally it should conform to the moral views of what is right and wrong. However there will be situations where the law is narrower than what is considered morally correct. For example there is no law which makes it illegal for a person to have an affair outside marriage, although there is provision for divorce and family property and children to be protected. Many would however see the 'guilty' person as being immoral. In contrast to park on double yellow lines is illegal, but not everyone would see this act as immoral.

What is ethically right to an individual depends upon their cultural and ethnic background and their upbringing and religious views. It is a very personal matter.

There could be occasions where the law permits an activity which is seen by some to be immoral. One example of this is a termination of pregnancy. As will be seen from Chapter 25 of the textbook and Section 10 of this unit, the Abortion Act 1967 provides a conscientious objection clause which enables a practitioner to refuse to participate in a termination of pregnancy, but this does not apply in an emergency situation where serious harm to the mother may occur if the termination is not carried out. There is a similar conscientious objection clause in the Human Fertilization and Embryology Act 1990.

Two recent books discuss the dual dimension of law and ethics by looking at specific themes, sometimes taking case studies and comparing them from an ethical and legal perspective. Whilst neither are specifically directed to midwives, some of the topics discussed are relevant to the midwife and this course and can be used to supplement this unit. The books are:

1. Fletcher, N., Holt, J. (1995). *Ethics, Law and Nursing.* Manchester: Manchester University Press.

2. Tingle, J., Cribb, A. (1995). *Nursing Law and Ethics.* Oxford: Blackwell Scientific.

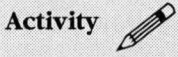

Activity | **Timing for this activity will depend on you**

Take any topic where there is an interesting legal/ethical dimension such as consent, confidentiality, termination, telling the truth to patients. By following your chosen topic in the textbook and the books on law and ethics cited above, list the legal issues and the ethical issues separately. Where do you personally stand on the issue?

This exercise will be a suitable one to extend into an essay which would give you the opportunity to demonstrate your academic ability. This kind of evidence would be necessary for APEL requirements.

Commentary
This is a difficult activity and one which could be repeated after you have studied the relevant section of law later on in this unit. It is important to be aware of the law on any specific topic and to understand where your own ethical views may diverge.

Professional issues, ethics and the law

As you will have seen from the above, the Codes issued by the UKCC are not the law, but they are part of what would be considered to be ethical practice. A midwife might find that there is a conflict in instructions which she has received from her employer and the standard she is expected to follow in complying with the UKCC codes. In Section 7 we consider the topic of whistle blowing and possible conflicts which might arise.

Endnote

Now that you have completed this section you should be able to answer the following questions. If you are uncertain read through Chapters 12 and 13 in the main textbook and then this section again, and ensure that you are confident before you proceed with the next section which is concerned with professional accountability.

Self-assessment questions

- How can you tell the difference between a criminal wrong and a civil wrong?
- What is the significance of precedent and hierarchy to the common law?
- What is the difference between a barrister and a solicitor?
- What is meant by the following terms: vicarious, prima facie, statute and ex gratia?
- Will breaking the law always be unethical?

References

Dimond, B. (1994). *Legal Aspects of Midwifery*. Hale: Books for Midwives Press.
UKCC (1992). *Code of Professional Conduct*. London: UKCC.
UKCC (1993). *Midwives Rules*. London: UKCC.
UKCC (1994). *The Midwife's Code of Practice*. London: UKCC.

SECTION TWO

Professional Accountability

On completion of this section you should have:

- Further developed your knowledge of personal professional responsibilities and knowledge of the Rules and Codes underpinning and advising midwifery practice.

- Developed a personal action plan to encourage the promotion of an effective professional relationship with your preceptor and/or supervisor of midwives.

This section includes an assessment opportunity. This could be suitable for AP(E)L assessment.

Alternatively this assessment may be used as the summative assessment for a distance learning module.

SECTION TWO

Professional Accountability

In this section we look at the professional role of the midwife, her relationship with her supervisor and the local supervising authority. We also consider the role of the professional conduct committee and the function and constitution of the UKCC. Now read Chapters 1–4 of the textbook before commencing this section.

Rules and Codes of Conduct

Midwives are one of the few professions who have Rules set out by statutory instrument which regulate their activities. In contrast to the Code of Professional Conduct (1992) and the Midwife's Code of Practice (1994), the Midwives Rules (1993) are part of the law and must be followed. Set out on p. 8 of Chapter 1 of the textbook are the duties of the UKCC to make rules regulating the practice of midwives.

Activity   **1 hour**

You are the ward manager responsible for interviewing two candidates for an integrated midwifery post within your NHS Trust.

- List the evidence you will require from the candidates to ensure they are eligible to practice as a midwife.
- How can you verify this is correct information?
- What should you do if you are in doubt about the validity of the information?

Commentary
Before you become responsible for the interviewing and selection of staff make sure that you have received suitable training and support from your line manager and Trust personnel and training department. Find out what recruitment and selection policies are in use before you take on these responsibilities (read Chapter 21 for more details).

- Check UKCC PIN number. Ring 0171 6377181 to confirm the name and number are on the 'live' register. The UKCC issue organizations with caller-code and password prior to confirmation being provided.
- Check the originals of all certificates and registration documents.

- Have sight of the candidates personal professional profile (see Table 1.10 on p. 12 of textbook).
- Make sure you have references from reliable sources.
- Remember the recommendations of the Clothier Report (see Table 13.4 on p. 138 of the textbook).

Local supervising authority

From the Rules and the Codes you will see that the local supervising authority is given clear duties in relation to the supervision of the midwife, suspension from practice and the provision of information. These functions are shown on pp. 14–22 of the textbook.

Activity 2 hours

The 1992 Act made changes to the duty (see p. 19 Table 2.6) to provide information. Obtain from your local supervising authority any policies and documents it has issued relating to midwives, supervisors and midwifery practice.

Then prepare for the chief executive of the new health authority a protocol setting out the role of the LSA, its constitution and purpose. Assess this critically and make recommendations on any revisions to these duties which you consider would be of advantage.

Commentary

This should have been a useful activity in ensuring that you have at your finger tips all the relevant information in relation to the LSA and all local policies. You should follow up this activity by identifying any gaps in the existing policies and discuss with your supervisor who would have the responsibility for filling these gaps. The exercise is of particular importance in view of the organizational changes in the NHS which came into effect in April 1996, when in England the duties of the LSA, formerly undertaken by the Regional Health Authority devolved to the new health authorities at district level.

Midwives and supervision

As you will see from Chapter 2 there is considerable controversy at present over the role and future developments which should take place in the function of the supervisor of midwives. The supervisor of midwives may or may not be the manager of the midwife. The midwife should find that her supervisor is of considerable support to her, especially when she is concerned about the service provided to the mother.

Activity   2 hours

(There are two parts to this activity; only the first part has been timed)

Part 1
- Study the duties of the supervisor of midwives and the responsibilities of the midwife as outlined in the Rules and the Codes.
- Undertake a strength, weakness, opportunities and threats (SWOT) analysis of the relationship which exists between yourself and your supervisor.
- In the light of the results of this SWOT analysis, draw up an action plan to make the relationship more effective.

Part 2 of this activity depends on your needs identified above.

Discuss the results with your supervisor of midwives.

Those student midwives who do not yet have a supervisor of midwives could carry out a theoretical exercise to determine the value of the supervisor/midwife system and decide whether any changes should be made to the present relationship and duties. This exercise should include a plan for making effective use of their designated supervisor of midwives once the student is qualified.

The timing of this activity depends on you.

This exercise would be suitable for assessment at level 3 if it included a literature search and you present recommendations that draw on currently available evidence.

Commentary

Midwives are unique amongst registered health professionals in having a long established system of statutory supervision. Clinical supervision systems are now being developed by other practitioners registered with the UKCC and midwives can be proactive in such developments. The debate surrounding the midwifery supervision (clinical and statutory function) is ongoing.

Obtain a copy of the UKCC Position statement on clinical supervision for nursing and health visiting (UKCC, April 1996).

In Appendices 2 and 3 you will find two examples of forms that midwives are currently using to identify legal and professional issues.

Appendix 2 is a form designed to assist supervisors of midwives to determine the possible allegations which may arise from an incident related to midwifery practice. The use of such a tool could be beneficial for any practitioner who needs to determine the professional/legal issues which may be drawn upon from a critical incident.

This form was developed by Kate Harmond, a midwife who acts as an advisor to the NHS Executive (South Thames). The authors are grateful for her permission to use and adapt this material.

Appendix 3 is a form which midwives have used successfully in helping them monitor and identify legal issues which maybe challenged when developing new services, practice developments or wishing to systematically review a significant incident.

Please note
If you choose to use these forms as tools to assist identification of possible legal issues which have or may be challenged, remember that it is important that appropriate support networks exist so that any problems identified can be dealt with.

Another source of information relating to the role of the supervisor of midwives is the distance learning pack developed by the English National Board of the UKCC (1992).

There is also an additional module currently under development.

Currently the role of the supervisor of midwives is under scrutiny from researchers in England and Wales. Both reports will be available in 1997.

Professional conduct proceedings

Chapter 3 of the textbook covers the role of the UKCC in the maintenance of professional standards and the procedure and powers of the preliminary proceedings committee and the professional conduct committee. Supplement this chapter with reference to the UKCC summary of the procedure. Refer also to diagram provided by the UKCC (1993) which sets out the procedure in a flow-diagram (Appendix 5).

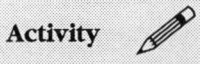

> **Activity** — **1 hour**
>
> You are told by a midwife colleague that she has been reported to the UKCC because she gave an incorrect dose of naloxone hydrochloride to a baby requiring resuscitation at birth.
>
> - Can the supervisor of midwives suggest a period of supervised practice?
> - Should this be resolved at local level and do the mechanisms exist for this?
> - If this case is referred to the Professional Conduct Committee what information should the midwife have prepared?
> - What information should the Supervisor of Midwives have prepared and likewise what information should the manager make available?
>
> Assist this midwife in preparing her for the format that the investigation by the UKCC will take. Advise her on the various stages. Consider the implications of a professional conduct committee hearing. Consider such issues as:
>
> - the defences available to her
> - the evidence she would need to collate
> - what form of representation she should have
> - possible sources of advice.

Suggestion
Use the form (Appendix 2) to guide your systematic evaluation of the incident.

Commentary
It is difficult to prepare a case in the abstract but this activity should familiarize you with the procedure of the UKCC. Note that the starting point of every investigation is 'Has there been misconduct by a midwife?'. Misconduct is defined as 'conduct unworthy of a midwife'. This definition gives scope for the current attitudes on the expected standards of a midwife both professionally and personally to be taken into account. Thus misconduct could relate to actions not directly connected with work such as failure to pay a parking fine, shop lifting, a breach of the peace with neighbours.

Attending a PCC hearing

If you have the opportunity to visit a professional conduct committee hearing of the UKCC you would be well advised to take it, since seeing a hearing, the way the evidence is given, the procedure which is followed gives a very good picture of the control of the standards of the registered practitioners.

The UKCC regularly advertise in the nursing and midwifery press when such meetings and professional conduct committee's are being held in your locality. Alternatively you could contact UKCC headquarters enquiring when such meetings are planned.

Legal Aspects of Midwifery Workbook

Contact address and telephone numbers:
United Kingdom Central Council for Nursing, Midwifery and Health Visiting, 23 Portland Place, London W1N 4JT (Tel: 0171 637 7181, Fax: 0171 436 2924).

Post Registration Education and Practice (PREP)

Midwives will note that transitional arrangements have been introduced to bring midwifery professional update requirements to a minimum of five days every three years. Midwives have always had a professional and personal duty to maintain their competence and attend refresher study days. They should also ensure that they compile a personal profile which can be used to illustrate areas where they need and have acquired additional training and support.

Activity — 2 hours

In the light of the transitional arrangements in relation to PREP (see p. 12 of the textbook) and the Midwives Rules and the Codes of Practice draw up a protocol to guide midwives in ensuring that the competence of the midwife is maintained and that she is able to reregister every three years. The protocol can be based on a particular area of activity such as births at home, water births or some other new developments. Alternatively it can cover the role of the midwife in general terms.

Commentary
This activity should be of practical help to you in ensuring that you maintain your competence to practice. You should use the profile that you are required to keep to ensure that you identify areas where you need to revise your practice and ensure safe development of practice, plus evidence of appropriate updating and education.

Appendix 4 is an example of a self review form developed for midwives to enable them to identify practice and personal development needs. Your identified needs could become the focus of discussion with your clinical supervisor/supervisor of midwives.

Endnote

You have now completed an introduction to the role of the midwife, the supervisor of midwives and the function of the UKCC in maintaining the professional standard of practitioners.

Before you move onto the next section covering client centred care, answer the questions set out to ensure that you have an understanding of this section. Reread the textbook for any issues which you cannot recall.

Self-assessment questions

- What is the difference between the Rules and the Codes in terms of legal status?
- Identify the role of the local supervising authority. If you are a supervisor of midwives prepare an information letter to midwives outlining the changes occurring following the changes to the RHAs, DHAs and FHSAs.
- Which body forms the Local Supervising Authority?
- Identify five statutory functions of the supervisor of midwives.
- What is the difference between the Preliminary Proceedings Committee and the Professional Conduct Committee?
- How is misconduct defined?

References

Dimond, B. (1994). *Legal Aspects of Midwifery.* Hale: Books for Midwives Press.

ENB (1992). *Preparation of Supervisors of Midwives: Open Learning programme.* London: ENB.

Harmond, K. (1995). *Local Supervising Authorities for Midwives: Guidance for Midwives, Managers, Health Professionals and Consumers.* London: South Thames Regional Health Authority.

UKCC (1992). *Code of Professional Conduct.* London: UKCC.

UKCC (1993). *Complaints about Professional Conduct.* London: UKCC.

UKCC (1993). *Midwives Rules.* London: UKCC.

UKCC (1994). *The Midwife's Code of Practice.* London: UKCC.

UKCC (1996). *Position Statement on Clinical Supervision for Nurses and Health Visitors.* London: UKCC.

SECTION THREE

Client Centred Care, Consent to Treatment and Information Giving

On completion of this section you should be able to:

- Understand the law related to trespass to the person.

- Actively reflect upon your practice, analysing methods of giving and receiving information.

SECTION THREE

Client Centred Care, Consent to Treatment and Information Giving

After studying this section you should be able to understand the law relating to trespass to the person, and the duty to give information to patients. You should also have an understanding of the nature of consent and the situations in which treatment can be given without consent. Practical activities will require your looking critically at the use of birth plans and communication with the client.

'Changing Childbirth'

The aim of the recommendations of 'Changing Childbirth' (1993) is to ensure greater involvement of the mother in the decisions made at every stage of the pregnancy and postnatal care.

Activity — **3 hours**

Read Chapter 5 on Woman Centred Care (pp. 52–58) of the textbook and undertake the following tasks.

1. Study Table 5.2 on page 54 which gives the indicators of success set by the report on 'Changing Childbirth'.

   - How many of these are now achieved in your area?
   - What action would be required to implement those targets which are not already achieved?
   - What audit mechanisms exist to monitor that the targets continue to be attained and improved upon?
   - Are there any other indicators which you consider could be used to identify the extent to which childbirth is woman centred?
   - What are the dangers in establishing and monitoring a limited range of targets?

Commentary
This activity may be time consuming. This will depend on your level of knowledge, access to local audit mechanisms and the involvement of consumer representatives in local planning.

Current initiatives related to the clinically effective use of resources, personnel and evidence-based care are directed at the commissioners of health care, providers of services and the different professions which should be involved in these initiatives. Midwives should be able to apply their knowledge of professional and legal issues to providing clinically effective care.

Activity — **30 minutes**

Return to Chapter 5 in the textbook.

The chapter considers the issue of choices to be made by a woman during pregnancy and the need to involve the woman in decision making.

Discuss with a colleague how you would distinguish between a need, a want or a demand (see Naidoo, J., Wills, J. [1994]. *Health Promotion; Foundations for Practice.* London: Bailliere Tindall Ltd.)

Map out the choices which could occur at various stages of the pregnancy and consider the extent to which the availability of choice is restricted by financial, organization, cultural or other reasons.

Commentary
In January 1996 a collaborative initiative from the NHS Centre for Reviews and Dissemination and MIDIRS was launched. This is entitled Informed Choice Information. These leaflets are designed to provide up-to-date information to women and professionals. For further information contact: Informed Choice, PO Box 669, Bristol BS99 5FG.

These activities should enable you to look critically at your practice in terms of the involvement and the relationship between midwife and mother. Often realizing the full autonomy of the mother is more an attitude of mind rather than practical regulation but the law sets the framework and sanctions and it is the law of trespass to which we now turn.

Trespass to the person
Chapter 6 sets out the law relating to trespass to the person, which can be brought by an individual who claims that they have been touched without her consent or other lawful justification. Note the following characteristics of an action for trespass to the person.

- Harm does not have to be shown: the action is established if there is an unauthorized touching (i.e. one without consent or other justification recognized by the law).

- The motive in assisting the person is irrelevant. It is no defence to say that the treatment was given in order to benefit the patient, if the mother had refused to give consent.

Activity — **30 minutes**

Read Chapter 6 and analyse your practice in terms of the types of treatment and care given to the mother (Table 6.1 given on p.59 gives some examples of treatments but this is by no means comprehensive).

List the various forms of care and treatment which may be given and alongside each record the nature of consent which is given. See example below.

Treatment:
caesarean section

Nature of consent
written consent
consent by word of mouth

Birth plans

The textbook considers that these should not be regarded as actual consent to various treatments but as part of the communication and planning between midwife and mother about the pregnancy birth and postnatal care.

Activity — **1 hour**

Either: Obtain a copy of a birth plan completed in respect of a mother who has already been confined.

Discuss with the midwife who was responsible for her care the extent to which the birth plan was useful in structuring the communication between midwife and mother. Was the midwife aware of any differences between the mother's plan and the actual care and treatment? Were any modifications necessary?

Or: Draft a list of topics upon which you would wish to focus discussion with a mother, at an appropriate time during the antenatal period.

This could form the basic elements of a birth plan. How can you ensure that the midwife's need to act according to her professional standards should be protected in the birth plan?

Legal Aspects of Midwifery Workbook

Commentary

You will be able to establish any weaknesses in your plan or list of topics for discussion by reflecting on your clinical practice.

Remember that women are entitled to unbiased information upon which they can make informed choices regarding their care.

Acting without consent

Pages 72-77 of the textbook discuss the situations in which treatment can be given without the consent of the mother. The most important of these as far as the midwife is concerned is situations of necessity. Thus if the mother was unconscious or for other reasons unable to give consent, the midwife would be able to provide treatment for her, acting in the mother's best interests following the Bolam Test. This is the basis of the decision made by the House of Lords in the case of *Re F* (see pp. 72–73). In the case of *Re T* the Court of Appeal emphasized the importance of the professional ensuring that a refusal was valid. In that case, (see pp. 71–72) the Court of Appeal held that the woman had not given a valid refusal and blood could therefore be administered to her without her consent.

The case of *Re S* where a woman was compelled to undergo a caesarean section without her consent has caused much debate and consternation amongst midwives and client representative groups. Note from Table 6.8 (p. 76 of textbook) the conclusions of the ethics committee of the Royal College of Obstetricians and Gynaecologists that it would not encourage its members to seek a court declaration in favour of treatment being given if a competent mother refused consent to lifesaving treatment. The corollary of this is that there may be some preventable deaths of mothers and babies.

Activity   **15 minutes**

What records would you need to keep if you were aware that a mother was refusing to give consent to treatment and you realized that this may involve a life and death situation? Who would you inform if caring for a mother refusing consent for treatment?

Commentary

Your answer should include not only records relating to the views of the mother and identification of the specific treatments discussed but any facts relating to her competence and the basis of her decisions.

Information given to the patient

If consent is given by the mother, she cannot bring an action for trespass to the person, but she may be able to sue in negligence for breach of the duty of care. This duty of care, which is explained fully in Chapter 13 of the textbook and in Section 5 of this workbook, includes the duty to give information to the patient. This duty is discussed in Chapter 7.

In contrast to an action for trespass to the person, where treatment is given without consent, in an action of breach of the duty of care in failing to provide sufficient information, the person bringing an action must show that harm has occurred.

Activity 1 hour

Examine the types and nature of the information which is given to the mother during the pregnancy and then answer the following questions:

- To what extent do you consider that this is sufficient to ensure that she is able to make a reasonable decision?
- Do you consider that the information could be made more client friendly?
- Are there any gaps in the information which is given?
- What kinds of information is given in writing and what is given by word of mouth? What should be the balance between the two?
- What attention is given to the ethnic and cultural needs of women in your area? Is everything available to them in translation?
- Is the information evidence-based and are all those providing care aware of the evidence?

Take any area of current controversy, e.g. the use of ultrasound, the administration of Vitamin K, and obtain the prevailing views on the advice and action which should be taken. Then draft how the conflicting information could be conveyed to the mother, so that she can make a reasonable decision. How would you record the discussion and the outcome?

Summary

Midwives should ensure that they involve the mothers in every decision which has to be made during the pregnancy and obtain a valid consent.

Where the midwife is justified in acting without the consent of the mother she should identify the legal reason which enables her to act in this way.

Easily understood comprehensive information should be available to the mother and the midwife should herself ensure that she is aware of and keeps up to date with current developments.

Endnote

Before you move on to Section 4 which covers records, confidentiality and access to health information, look again at Chapters 5, 6 and 7 of the textbook and ensure that you have fulfilled the aims set at the beginning of this section. Test yourself by answering the following questions.

> **Self-assessment questions**
>
> - Name any five indicators of success identified in the 'Changing Childbirth' Report.
> - What is meant by a trespass to the person?
> - What is the legal status of a birth plan?
> - In what circumstances could treatment be given without the consent of the mother?
> - What information would you give to a 40-year-old pregnant mother about the advantages and disadvantages of the available prenatal tests?

References

Dimond, B. (1994). *Legal Aspects of Midwifery*. Hale: Books for Midwives Press.

Department of Health (1993). *Changing Childbirth: Report of Expert Maternity Group*. London: HMSO.

Naidoo, J., Will, J. (1994). *Health Promotion*. London: Bailliere Tindall Ltd.

SECTION FOUR

Records, Confidentiality and Access

This section enables you to explore:

- The notion of confidentiality and the professional duty to maintain the woman's right to confidentiality.

- Identify areas within midwifery practice where the disclosure of information is justified within the law.

- The required standards of record keeping and critically evaluate local/personal standards.

SECTION FOUR

Records, Confidentiality and Access

In this section we look at the mother's rights in relation to access to records and at the duty of confidentiality owed to her by the midwife. In addition we consider the ways in which records are used and how standards can be improved. Chapters 9, 10 and 14 in the textbook apply.

Confidentiality

The professional duty to maintain the confidentiality of information about the mother/client is well recognized. The UKCC clearly sets out the duty in the recently published 'Guidelines to Professional Practice' (UKCC, 1996). This document has been circulated to every midwife registered with the UKCC. In addition midwives may find that their employers have included a confidentiality clause in their contracts of employment. Even if it is not explicitly set out, the courts might well imply such a term as part of the duty of loyalty owed by the employee to the employer (see Section 6 for a discussion on employment law).

The remedies which are available if this duty of confidentiality is broken are shown in Figure 4.1.

- Breach of duty of care to maintain confidentiality
- Breach of trust
- Disciplinary proceedings by employer
- Professional Conduct proceedings by UKCC
- Complaint through the statutory complaints machinery
- Injunction to stop a threatened breach
- Criminal proceedings where the breach is a criminal offence.

Fig. 4.1: Remedies for breach of confidentiality

Records, Confidentiality and Access

> **Activity** ✏️ ⏲️ **The time for this activity will vary**
>
> How good are you at maintaining the confidentiality of information about the mother/client? During a week's work keep account of the occasions on which you pass on information about the woman noting the following:
>
> | **type of information** | **to whom disclosed** | **reason** |
> | e.g. clinical, social etc. | professional | |
>
> Be as comprehensive as you can, recording the event even if you have not mentioned the name, and including social occasions such as meal times when you are discussing your work with colleagues.

Note: when you undertake this activity ensure that you do not record any information by which the event or persons can be recognized.

Commentary

If you have been able to complete this activity fully, you might be surprised at the frequency that information is passed on about the client. The next stage is to consider when the reasons for the disclosure justify the breach of confidentiality in law.

> **Activity** 📖 ⏲️ **15 minutes**
>
> Read pp. 91–95 of the textbook and in the light of your answers to the activity above decide what category, if any, your reason for disclosure comes under.

Commentary

You will probably find that the most frequent justification for passing on confidential information is 'in the interests of the client'. This can justify notifying other members of the midwifery and multi-disciplinary team about aspects of the mother which they need to know in order to be able to provide her with appropriate care. Note that the court can order the disclosure of information and does not recognize any refusal based on the fact that the information has been obtained through professional confidences. If the information is relevant to an issue being considered by the court, then unless it has been provided between client and lawyer as part of the litigation process, or the government requires it to be withheld on grounds of national security in the public interest, it can be ordered to be disclosed.

Disclosure in the public interest

This is one of the most difficult exceptions to the duty of confidentiality. Read the UKCC advice in its 'Guidelines of Professional Practice' (UKCC, 1996) and note its suggested procedure for ensuring that such disclosure is justified. From the textbook note the two cases where the defence of disclosure in the public interest was discussed.

Activity — **1 hour**

Consider the following situations and decide if disclosure should be made on the basis of the public interest. Identify to whom, if anyone, the disclosure could be made and what you would record to justify your action.

Situation	Reason	Record

- The mother is a drug addict
- A child in the family is withdrawn and covered with bruises
- The mother tells you that her husband is physically violent towards her
- You discover that stolen goods are being stored in the house
- The mother tells you she is HIV positive
- The mother tells you that the pregnancy is the result of IVF
- The mother tells you that she is carrying the baby as a surrogate for her sister
- The path lab results show that the mother has tested positive for a sexually transmitted disease
- A colleague tells you that two earlier children of the mother are in care of the local authority
- The mother has a history of psychiatric illness requiring in-patient care.

Commentary

Whenever you pass on confidential information, you should be able to justify what legal reason would be recognized for the disclosure, why disclosure was permissible to the particular person and the extent of the information disclosed. Your records should give all this information.

Access to records

Read pp. 95–98 of the textbook. From this you will see that there are several laws relating to the right of a client to obtain access to her records. However none of these give an absolute right and access can be withheld if access would cause serious harm to the physical or mental health of the patient or another person or the identity of a third person who did not wish to be identified would be disclosed. (This latter reason for refusing to allow access does not apply if the third person is a health professional caring for the patient.)

Records, Confidentiality and Access

| Activity | untimed activity |

Midwifery departments, especially the antenatal departments, were among the first to permit client held records and allow full access. One of the key targets and indicators of success of the 'Changing Childbirth' report is that all women should be entitled to carry their own notes (see Section 3 of this pack and p. 54 of the textbook).

- Look at the situation in your own practice. Do you have a policy of open access? Do mothers carry their own records?
- If you do, what difficulties are associated with this scheme? What are the advantages?
- If such a scheme is not in existence, how could it be implemented? What difficulties would you envisage and how could these be overcome?

Obtain a copy of any leaflet prepared in your hospital/unit for mothers. What does it say about access to records? How client friendly is the leaflet? If such a leaflet does not exist, consider how one could be drafted and what should be the minimum contents.

Standards of record keeping

It is anticipated that one of the results of a legal right of the mother to access her health records is that the standard of record keeping should improve.

| Activity | 2 hours |

Read Chapter 14 pp. 149–56 of the textbook and reread the UKCC advisory paper 'Standards for Records and Record keeping' (1993).

List errors which you have noted in record keeping and compare your list with those shown in the UKCC paper. Then turn to the check list in Table 14.3 p. 156 of the textbook and apply it to your own practice.

Look up some records which you completed about a year ago and (if possible with a colleague) imagine that you are now being called to give evidence in court about your professional practice with that mother. How far will the records enable you to answer any detailed questions on what you did or did not do? (If you are able to do this activity with a colleague, the colleague could ask you questions on your records.)

Commentary

Those practitioners who have been called to give evidence in court, whether a coroner's inquest, civil or criminal court or industrial tribunal or professional conduct proceedings will be aware of the dependence upon good, clear comprehensive records in being able to give evidence. Monitoring the standards of your record keeping should be a regular activity. If this is undertaken on a routine basis with colleagues, improvements can be made and standards maintained.

Complaints

Chapter 10 of the textbook describes the procedure for handling complaints and sets out the recommendations of the Wilson report 'Being Heard'.

Activity   **untimed activity**

Read Chapter 10 and obtain a copy of your unit's complaints policy and leaflet.

Discuss with colleagues any recent complaints which have been made in your department and try and trace the procedure which has been followed. To what extent are the Wilson principles set out in Table 10.3 on p. 100 implemented in your unit. Ask the designated officer for handling complaints in your unit for a copy of the last report sent to the Board on complaints. (This should include the time which elapses between the complaint first being received and the final letter of explanation being sent.)

Commentary

It takes courage for a person to make a complaint, especially where she is dependent upon the services of the staff. Encouraging mothers to make suggestions for the improvement of the services and to voice their concerns is an important part of the midwife's work. Client feed back is essential to ensure that the principles of 'Changing Childbirth' are being implemented. Fear of criticism can lead to defensive practice and an unwillingness to consider the possibility of improving the service. A high level of complaints does not necessarily mean that the service is inferior to that provided where fewer complaints are made, it might reflect upon an organization which is more open to suggestions and could therefore be a positive sign. It is important however to ensure that complaints are followed up and any justified criticisms leads to improvements.

- Also be aware of any issues which arise from collaborative care planning where multidisciplinary members share the same medical records.
- Use of computers for the recording of information is common place, are there any guidelines regarding the access to computer stored data?

Endnote

This section has covered different topics relating to record keeping and the duty of confidentiality owed to the client. Before you move onto the next section which deals with civil liability and the civil wrong of negligence, answer the following questions to ensure that you understand and remember the basic principles of the section.

Self-assessment questions

- Where does the duty to maintain confidentiality come from?
- What is meant by the public interest?
- What other exceptions does the law recognize to the duty of confidentiality?
- What is the difference between a statutory right of access to health records and an informal right?
- Name six principles of good standards of record keeping.

References

Dimond, B. (1994). *Legal Aspects of Midwifery*. Hale: Books for Midwives Press.
Department of Health (1994). *Being Heard: The Report of a Review Committee on NHS Complaints Procedures*. London: HMSO.
UKCC (1993). *Standards for Records and Record Keeping*. London: UKCC.
UKCC (1996). *Guidelines to Professional Practice*. London: UKCC.

SECTION FIVE

Civil Liability: Negligence

This section enables you to:

- Examine the law related to the tort of negligence.

- Evaluate critically local protocols and standards of care.

SECTION FIVE

Civil Liability: Negligence

This section looks at the law relating to the tort (i.e. civil wrong) of negligence and the procedure which takes place in the civil courts. Chapters 12 and 13 of the textbook cover the topic and include a review of the law in specific situations.

There is no doubt that litigation in health care is increasing and that civil claims over maternity services can result in the highest awards of compensation.

Activity 30 minutes

A. Read pp. 113–22 in the textbook which sets out the basic principles of the civil action for negligence. Note that any person seeking compensation for personal injury or death must prove the following elements of negligence:

- duty of care
- breach of the duty of care
- causation
- harm.

Each of these elements is explained and illustrated in the text. Now look at the following situations and decide if there is likely to be a successful action.

Activity 1 hour

Write your answers down, examining whether each of the required elements would appear to be present. Identify the evidence which you consider the plaintiff (i.e. the person bringing the civil action) would need to show in order to succeed in the action being brought.

- A mother complains of waiting an excessive length of time in the antenatal department.
- A mother claims that her shirodkar suture was not removed in time and she has suffered internal injury.
- A baby is found to be brain damaged.
- A mother loses some personal possessions, whilst in the antenatal clinic.
- A midwife on holiday is on the beach, when she discovers that a pregnant sunbather appears to have gone into premature labour.
- A midwife is delayed by a road accident in attending a mother who planned for the birth at home. When she arrives the baby is born with the umbilical cord around his neck. Unfortunately the baby does not survive.

Legal Aspects of Midwifery Workbook

> **Activity (continued)** 🕐 **1 hour**
>
> B. Look at the cases described in full in the text: *Hinfey* v. *Salford Health Authority* on pp. 141-45 and *Whitehouse* v. *Jordan* on pp. 146–48 and identify the same four elements and the evidence which was discussed.

Commentary

In each of your answers you should have been able to state whether or not the four elements appeared to be present. The examples of decided cases will show the type of detail which will be relevant in a court action in deciding what took place and whether the plaintiff can prove her case.

Standards of care

It will have been noted from the text that the courts apply the Bolam test to decide if there has been a failure to provide the reasonable standard of care. How does the Bolam Test relate to local standards, protocols and procedures? Local protocols should reflect the professional standards which the mother is entitled to expect. They may be higher than is normally provided – they cannot be lower.

Read offprint 'Complementary therapy and the midwife' (p. 109 of this workbook) – this article illustrates how evidence of competance and standards of care are essential when the legal implications of new practices and treatments offered are given due consideration.

> **Activity** 🕐 **Time for this activity may vary**
>
> Take any procedure which is regularly undertaken at work, for example:
>
> - the care of a woman admitted with a threatened abortion at 22 weeks gestation;
> - 'routine' fetal monitoring for all women for 30 minutes on admissions to labour ward;
> - withholding food from women in labour.
>
> Ascertain if there are any locally agreed protocol covering different procedures. Consider to what extent it would accord with the standard followed elsewhere. To what extent is your practice based on this protocol. Note the case of *Maynard* v. *West Midlands Health Authority* discussed on p. 116 and the fact that there can be divergences from the usually accepted standard if special circumstances exist.

Defences

Pages 124–129 cover the different defences which may be relevant when a case is brought. The burden is usually upon the plaintiff to establish the elements of negligence unless the situation known as res ipsa loquitur occurs. This is described on p. 120.

Many cases are decided entirely on the facts, i.e. if the plaintiff can establish through witnesses and other evidence that the defendant is in breach of the duty of care which was owed and that this breach of duty caused reasonably foreseeable harm, then the plaintiff will win.

Limitation of time

Of particular difficulty in cases brought in relation to midwifery or obstetric care is the fact that if the action is brought in the name of the baby, time does not start to run i.e. the limitation of the time for initiating the action, does not begin until the child is 18 years. In the case of brain-damaged babies, there is no time limit within which the action must be brought until the child/adult dies. The implications of this for record keeping are clear. In Section 4 we considered the importance of record keeping and discuss in that context a case which was not heard till 16 years after the birth. This is not unusual.

From the perspective of the parent or child, the limitation of time for initiating the action provides time for a realistic assessment of the child's condition and potential to be made.

The procedure

Set out below are illustrations of the kinds of documents known as pleadings which would be prepared by solicitors and barristers during the preparation for the court hearing.

- The originating writ: this must be served within four months of the date of issue
- The statement of claim
- The defence
- Request for further and better particulars
- Interrogatories
- Discovery of documents
- Pre-trial review.

Activity — Untimed activity

Consider any situation where harm may have occurred to a mother or child and the possibility of litigation being commenced.

Identify what you would include in a statement if you were asked by the solicitor for your employer about details of what happened. What would you hope would be contained in the records?

Legal Aspects of Midwifery Workbook

Commentary

Unfortunately this exercise is not an academic one since midwives are increasingly likely to be facing a request for information about an incident or care in relation to a complaint, possible litigation, an unexpected death, or a disciplinary issue. The midwife might not herself be at fault but she may have to be providing evidence in relation to criticism of a colleague.

A midwife confronted with this situation may choose to approach her supervisor for assistance to identify the key elements required and essential details to be included. NHS trusts require employees to identify and notify managers of untoward incidents. This is a part of risk management procedures.

Special situations

In Chapter 13, six different special situations are discussed which are relevant to midwifery practice. These are by no means exhaustive.

Activity **Timing for this activity will vary**

Identify an area of special concern about your own professional practice or the context within which you work. For example:

- A woman refuses to have continuous cardiotocograph recordings even though the midwife has correctly identified signs of fetal distress.

- The obstetrician wants all the women under his care to have 'routine' anomaly scans at 17–18 weeks gestation. No consent is sought from the women concerned. The midwife offers information to the women thus providing the opportunity for women to consent to or refuse this particular method of prenatal screening.

- The midwife is aware of the paediatrician taking blood from a neonate suspected of having Down's syndrome. The parents have not been approached for consent to this procedure as he does not want to worry them unnecessarily.

- The intravenous infusion pump is continually setting off an alarm. When you investigate, the pump is found to be faulty and a colleague has continued to use the faulty electrical equipment.

Then answer the following questions:

- What is the nature of the duty of care owed to the mother and child in this context?
- Define the standard of care which should be provided.
- What harm may be caused by a breach of the standard of care?
- What records would you require to show that you followed the reasonable standard?
- What defences would be available if harm occurred?

Civil Liability: Negligence

You may photocopy the form in Appendix 3 to help you systematically evaluate your chosen area of concern. Remember that you should discuss your concerns with your supervisor of midwives and your manager.

Quantum

The amount of compensation payable to a successful plaintiff will relate to the extent and nature of harm which has been suffered. Pages 122–24 illustrate the kinds of elements which are taken into account in determining the amount of compensation. Sometimes a defendant might accept liability but dispute the amount of compensation which is claimed. Other times the amount of compensation may be agreed but liability disputed. Sometimes both may be in dispute.

Endnote

This section has covered a wide range of topics arising from an action for negligence. Read again Chapter 12 and 13 of the textbook to ensure that you understand the subject, then by using the self-assessment questions set below, test how well you have understand the material. Ensure that you are confident before proceeding with the next section on employment law.

Self-assessment questions:

- What are the four elements which the plaintiff has to prove in an action for negligence?
- What is meant by vicarious liability?
- Name five defences to an action for negligence.
- What are the time limits in bringing an action for negligence?
- What is meant by a res ipsa loquitur situation?

Reference

Dimond, B. (1995). 'Complementary therapy and the midwife'. *Modern Midwife*, Vol.5, No.2, pp.32–34.
Dimond, B. (1994). *Legal Aspects of Midwifery*. Hale: Books for Midwives Press.

SECTION SIX

Employment Law

On completion of this section you should be able to apply:

- The principles of employment law to various situations.

SECTION SIX

Employment Law

The relevant chapters in the textbook for this section are Chapter 21 which covers employment law and Chapter 22 which covers independent midwives.

The relationship of employer/employee

Most midwives are employees. A few, known as independent midwives, are self-employed (see later). The employment relationship brings rights and duties. Some of these are based on the contract of employment which is agreed by the parties, others arise from Acts of Parliament and are known as statutory duties. Some terms are implied by law. These sources of employment law are described on pp. 205-09.

> **Activity**   **1 hour**
>
> Obtain a copy of your contract of employment. Consider each of the terms and the source books to which it might refer (e.g. when Whitley Council conditions are part of the contract, there may be a reference to the staff grouping, grade and specific conditions which apply to the individual's contract).
>
> Identify whether the terms have been agreed specifically with you or arise from collective bargaining, or have been incorporated as a result of an Act of Parliament. Compare your contract with the list of terms which must be particularized in a written statement as set out in Table 21.3 (p. 206). Are there any terms which are in the table but not in your contract?

Local bargaining

One of the results of the introduction of the internal market in the NHS is that the Government has encouraged the development of local bargaining of terms and conditions of service.

Legal Aspects of Midwifery Workbook

> **Activity** — **Time for this activity will vary**
>
> Read the offprint referring to local bargaining (p. 114 of this workbook) and consider the ways in which you and your colleagues could prepare for local negotiation of your terms and conditions of work. What evidence do you think that you would require? How would you decide on representation of midwives? What information and flexibility do you consider you could give to your representative?

Commentary
Note the principles of contract law relating to the formation, performance and termination of the contract of employment. A specific principle of contract law is that one party to a contract cannot change the terms unilaterally without the other's consent. A job description is not part of the terms and the description of work activity could be changed as long as it is within the scope of the title and what was envisaged by the parties at the time the contract was agreed. It may sometimes occur that because of a change in the work situation, an employee is asked to undertake different work than that covered by the contract of employment. The employer cannot force the employee to accept the changed conditions. However the employee may be facing a redundancy situation and if the alternative work or situation is considered reasonable, the employee's refusal might result in neither the initial job being available nor the alternative work, nor redundancy payment. Redundancy is discussed below.

Statutory rights

These are rights bestowed on the employee by Act of Parliament and p. 209 indicates some of them.

> **Activity** — **1 hour**
>
> Select one of the following statutory rights:
>
> - Maternity rights
> - The right not to be unfairly dismissed
> - The right to receive a written statement of the terms of service.
>
> Obtain from the Department of Education and Employment leaflets relating to the right which you have chosen. Study the leaflet and then undertake the following exercise:
>
> - What does the right consist of?
> - How is it enforced?
> - What criteria of eligibility must the claimant prove (e.g. length of continous service)?

> • Does it overlap with any comparable rights which are given under the contract of employment? (e.g. some maternity benefits which are available as a result of the Trade Union and Labour Relations and Employee Rights Act 1993 are recognized in contracts of employment as a result of collective bargaining).

Commentary
Check your answers to these questions with the personnel office of your unit and make contact with that department to obtain information about any overlap between statutory rights and those which have already been agreed through collective bargaining. The usual situation is that the employee is able to select whichever right gives her the most benefit, but the employer can offset any payment in respect of the contractual right against any liability under the statute. The employee cannot obtain the benefit twice!

Industrial action
There is concern that the introduction of local bargaining might lead to an increase in industrial action. In 1995 the Government agreed to a national increase for midwives and nurses of one per cent and left each local NHS employer to agree additional increases of up to two per cent making a total three per cent. Some NHS trusts failed to agree local increases up to two per cent and there were discussions about midwives taking strike action. Any industrial action would have to be decided by balloting the local membership of each trade union/professional organization.

For example, the Royal College of Midwives held a national ballot of its members. The result of this was that the RCM did overturn its policy of 'no industrial action' but this meant that although the RCM did not endorse striking it did endorse action which fell short of this i.e. 'working to grade'. Any decision to take industrial action would need to be endorsed by RCM Council.

Strike action
This is a prima facie breach of the contract of employment, since the withdrawal of labour is a breach of the implied term that the employee will obey the reasonable instructions of the employer and be faithful and loyal to the employer. What if the midwife decides to withdraw her labour or work to rule?

This would be seen in law as a breach of contract. The courts have even held, where railway men followed the rule book to the letter thereby causing trains to be delayed, that the action amounted to the breach of an implied term that the employee would cooperate with the employer.

Normally a strike or working to rule would give the right to the employer to regard the contract as ended by the employee's action, but the law provides some protection for the employee and if only a few of the strikers are dismissed, then that is an unfair dismissal of those dismissed. Where all are dismissed, and then some of them reinstated, then that amounts to an unfair dismissal of those not reinstated. The employer is also able to dismiss employees who take part in unofficial industrial action.

Clearly it is not usually the employer's wish to sever the contracts of those who go on strike, nor is it the striker's wish to see the contract at an end, but rather to see an improvement in her conditions. The practical effect therefore of a strike is usually not the ending of the contract. Whether it is the most effective form of action is of course a different issue.

Industrial action

The law provides certain protection where independent trade union members take part in industrial action. This protection is known as trade union immunities. Recent changes have seen a narrowing of trade union protection and the definition of lawful industrial action which will attract the protection. To be lawful, industrial action must be preceded by a secret ballot and notice must be given to the employer. The 1993 Act gave a new right to the citizen who suffers harm as a result of unlawful industrial action and a Commissioner for Protection against unlawful industrial action has been established. This independent officer can pay and make arrangements for legal advice and representation to be made available to any person who is claiming that he or she has been or will be deprived of goods and services as the result of unlawful industrial action. If successful the individual can be granted a court order to restrain the unlawful industrial action.

Activity	Timing for this activity depends on you
Obtain leaflets from the Department of Education and Employment relating to the rights of trade unions and industrial action. Answer the following questions: • What is the difference between lawful and unlawful industrial action? • What protection does a trade union receive if the industrial action is defined as lawful? • What are the consequences of the industrial action being defined as unlawful?	

Employment Law

Race discrimination

Activity	Untimed activity

Obtain details from the Race Relations Office about its function and the law relating to unlawful discrimination on grounds of race.

Then discuss existing procedures used during the selection process including the advertisement, the short listing, the procedure at an interview and the final selection to ensure that there is no discrimination on grounds of race. Your personal office should be able to provide evidence of local procedures.

Sex discrimination

The restriction on the appointment of male midwives ended on 1 January 1984. From this time health authorities could employ male midwives but had to ensure that appropriate arrangements were made for women to have freedom of choice to be attended by a female midwife and to be chaperoned if they were attended by a male midwife. As you will see from the figures quoted on p. 215 of the textbook there are only a small number of male midwives on the register.

Independent midwives

Chapter 22 discusses the legal situation of independent midwives. Since they are usually self-employed they do not enjoy the statutory rights given to employees. They may however employ staff and they should therefore be familiar with the duties that an employer owes to an employee.

Activity	1 hour

In the light of the information given in Chapters 21 and 22 draw up a list of the differences between the situation of the employed midwife compared with that of the independent midwife.

47

Legal Aspects of Midwifery Workbook

Endnote

It is important that both the employed and the independent self-employed midwife understands the law relating to employment. Before you move to the next section that looks at health and safety law check with the following self-assessment questions that you understand the law and read again Chapters 21 and 22.

Self-assessment questions

- What is the difference between implied and express terms in a contract of employment?
- Name five statutory rights given to the employee.
- What is the significance of local collective bargaining to the midwife?
- When is industrial action lawful?
- Could an employer insist upon a mother accepting a male midwife?

References

Dimond, B. (1994). *Legal Aspects of Midwifery*. Hale: Books for Midwives Press.

Department of Health (1996). *Local Pay 1996/97: Guidance for Purchasers* EL(96)9. London: DOH.

SECTION SEVEN

Health and Safety Law

On completion of this section you should be able to demonstrate your understanding of:

- The duties placed upon the midwife in relation to health and safety.

- The duties placed upon the employer in relation to health and safety.

SECTION SEVEN

Health and Safety Law

The basic principles

This section uses the material to be found in Chapters 18 and 28 of the textbook. It will be noted that health and safety laws cover every aspect of professional practice:

- The Health and Safety Act 1974 and the regulations based upon that are enforced through the criminal courts by enforcement agencies such as the health and safety inspectorate, environmental health inspectors and the crown prosecution service.
- Many duties of the employer and employee in relation to health and safety derive from the common law and are incorporated into the contract of employment by the law implying terms. These implied terms are enforceable through the remedies deriving from contract law and if harm occurs the victim can sue in the civil courts. They may also be the subject of proceedings in an industrial tribunal if the employee alleges that she has been unfairly or constructively dismissed.
- Statutory duties created by the civil law. Some statutes such as the Occupier's Liability Act 1957 and the Consumer Protection Act 1987 create duties which are enforceable through the civil courts by the individual who has suffered harm.
- The UKCC has through its Code of Professional Conduct and the Midwife's Code of Practice placed duties on the practitioner in relation to health and safety. Failure to observe these requirements could result in the practitioner facing proceedings for misconduct i.e. conduct unworthy of a midwife.

Activity 📖 ⏱ **1 hour**

Take any incident which involved a health and safety situation, which could have given rise to serious harm, e.g. a mother slipping on the floor, a midwife injuring her back, a child falling in the antenatal clinic. In the light of the statutory and common law duties outlined in Chapter 18 set out the possible repercussions from such an incident.

Identify the agency or person taking action, the court in which the action would be held and the possible outcome.

Identify the evidence which the plaintiff or prosecutor would require to succeed in her action.

Commentary

As a result of this activity you should become aware of how the law overlaps and there may be several different actions arising in different courts. They will not necessarily have the same outcomes because of the different requirements in relation to the burden of proof i.e. the civil courts require proof on a balance of probabilities, the criminal courts require proof beyond reasonable doubt. In some health and safety prosecutions once the prosecutor has established the facts, the defendant can try to prove that he took all reasonable care to meet the statutory duties and has to establish this on a balance of probabilities. Before you finish with this activity, identify what action could have been taken to prevent that particular incident arising and define who would have been responsible.

Manual handling

As you will note from the text, in 1992 the European Community passed health and safety directions which required member states to introduce regulations. The 'six pack' regulations are shown in Table 18.6. One of these covers requirements relating to manual handling. Evidence from the Royal College of Midwives (see p. 180) has shown that midwives are vulnerable to risks of back injuries. Note the details relating to the statutory requirements set out on pp. 180-3.

Activity   ⏱ **3 hours**

Obtain from your employer a copy of the health and safety policy in relation to manual handling and any procedure which has been drawn up specifically in relation to your department. Note the summary of the Regulations on manual handling on p. 181:

- If possible avoid manual handling
- If not possible, make a suitable and sufficient assessment of any manual handling which cannot be avoided
- Reduce the risk of injury from the handling so far as is reasonable practicable
- Review the assessment.

1. Apply these stages to manual handling carried out by midwives.
2. Record the results of your assessment.
3. List the action which you consider is now necessary to reduce the risk of injury.

Follow the results of this activity through with your senior manager and discuss with her the possibility of incorporating your conclusions within the health and safety policy of the unit/department.

Infectious diseases and the midwife

Chapter 28 sets out the details of the laws relating to infectious diseases. Note the requirements under the Public Health legislation to notify the authorities of certain diseases. The midwife has a two-fold responsibility:

- On the one hand she must protect her client from cross-infection and ensure that she does not carry infections from one client to another. If she herself is suffering from a transmissible infection, she must ensure that her manager is notified and that she withdraws from work until such time as she is safe.

- On the other hand she must ensure that she takes precautions to ensure that she does not become infected from a client suffering from an infectious disease. She cannot however refuse to care for a client on the grounds that the client is suffering from an infectious disease.

Midwives are concerned about the possibility of infection from HIV positive patients or AIDS sufferers. Even if all pregnant women were required to carry out a test (which is not recommended), it would not be possible to be certain which ones were carriers because of the possibility of false negatives during the few months between infection and the disease showing in any blood test. Midwives therefore have to care for all mothers on the assumption that any one could be HIV positive or an AIDS sufferer.

Activity **Timing will vary**

Carry out an analysis of your practice on the assumption that every client was an HIV/AIDS sufferer. Identify all the risks which could arise and against each one decide on the action which is necessary to reduce the possibility of infection being passed. Take note of the form of the risk reduction:

- Does it require more protective clothing?
- Does it require a change of work practice?
- What changes are necessary to ensure the safety of staff?

Note that the employer is required by an implied term in the contract of employment to take reasonable care of the health and safety of employees. Consider the recommendations which result from your audit and decide which of the changes would be regarded as reasonable and give reasons.

Then discuss the results of this audit with your manager.

Commentary

The structure involved in this audit is comparable to any other audit carried out under health and safety regulations. It is therefore similar to the manual handling assessment carried out previously. From pp. 174-79 you will note the general principles set out in relation to any risk assessment at work. These principles could be applied to risks from violence, from dangerous substances, from slippages, and any other dangers at work.

The midwife and hepatitis

There is concern at present with the possibility that midwives may be carriers of infectious disease to the client. One of the most difficult to eradicate is hepatitis B. The current guidance of the NHS Management Executive on the protection of health care workers and patients from hepatitis B recommends that all health care personnel who have direct contact with blood or blood stained fluids or with patients' tissues should be immunized. There can be little doubt that the midwife would come within the category of health professional staff who work in exposure prone procedures. This guidance does not have legal force and the following questions arise: Can the midwife lawfully refuse to be tested or vaccinated?

Activity 1 hour

Answer the question as to whether the midwife could be compelled to accept vaccination in relation to both the employed and independent midwife, using the guidance contained in the NHS Executive circular.

Commentary

For employed midwives a distinction must be drawn between new staff and existing staff.

Paragraph 4 of Annex A (in the NHS circular) on the implementation of the guidance which covers new appointments states that:

> 'employers should make compliance with this guidance a condition of service for new staff appointed to posts which involve participation in "exposure prone procedures". Wherever possible, immunity/carrier status should be determined before their employment is confirmed.'

Such a requirement by an employer that a prospective employee should receive the necessary immunity against hepatitis B as a condition of obtaining employment is lawful. If the employee fails to comply with this condition, then the contract of employment ends or fails to commence (depending upon whether it was a condition precedent or a condition subsequent). Annex B sets out a flow chart for immunization and follow-up. If the appropriate clauses are included in the contract, the employer can also lawfully request new staff to comply with the requisite follow up procedures to ensure maximum immunity.

If the new staff member fails to comply with the immunization programme, then the contract could be lawfully terminated. The employee is in breach of an express term of the contract. It is probable that the employee would not be able to apply for unfair dismissal since she would not have the requisite length of continuous service of employment. If however an application to the industrial tribunal were available the employer would have to show that the breach of contract by the employee justified the dismissal of the employee.

Existing staff

Existing staff may not have a term in their contracts requiring them to be tested or vaccinated. Where such staff refused to comply with the implementation of the guidance, the employer would have to show that there is an implied term in the contract which would require staff to comply with such instructions on the grounds that they were reasonable orders.

The guidance states (paragraph 11 and 12 of Annex A) that:

> 'If a health care worker whose work involves "exposure prone procedures" refuses to comply with the guidance, he or she should be considered as if e-antigen positive and managed accordingly.
>
> NHS employers should involve their legal advisers in any case where a substantial legal difficulty arises in connection with the implementation of this guidance.'

Such a difficulty could be a member of staff refusing to be tested or to receive the appropriate vaccination.

It is clear that the employer does not have the power to compel the employee to be tested or to receive a vaccination. Such an action without the consent of the employee would be a trespass to his/her person. There is no legal power of the employer to insist upon such action.

Could the employer however give an order for the employee to receive a vaccination with the sanction that if the employee refused to comply, then the employee would face disciplinary proceedings and possibly dismissal? If such an instruction was deemed to be reasonable then the employee has a duty to obey it and could lawfully face disciplinary proceedings for failing to obey it.

Is a request by an employer that the employee be tested for hepatitis B and if necessary receive immunization reasonable?

The reasonableness of the request would depend upon the following:

- Is the employee in a high risk area (defined in the guidance as one whose work involves exposure prone procedures)?
- Are there any risks to the employee in being vaccinated or tested for hepatitis B?

- Could dangers to the employee and to the patient be significantly reduced by compliance with the guidance?
- Does the guidance meet the standards of the reasonable employer/practitioner?

On the basis of the present evidence it would appear that the answers to these questions is affirmative and that an instruction from the employer to be tested and, if necessary, to be vaccinated would be regarded by the courts as reasonable and therefore failure to comply with the instructions could result in disciplinary proceedings.

Alternatively failure by the employee to comply with the instructions could result in the employee being regarded as e-antigen positive and therefore being transferred to a non-exposure prone area of work. Paragraph 13 of Annex A suggests that the advice of a specialist occupational health physician should be sought about the work that an e-antigen positive carrier of the virus may continue to perform.

If such suitable alternative work was not available then the employer should consider the possibility of retraining, but eventually the employee could face dismissal.

However each case would have to be decided upon its own merits and facts. There may for example be some rare cases where an employee could establish that it would be unreasonable to request her to be vaccinated. It could be contraindicated for example by a severe reaction to vaccines. Paragraph 16 of Annex A deals with such a possibility and suggests that they should be checked to ensure that they are not e-antigen positive carriers of the virus. Regular testing may be considered.

Other reasons for refusal may include refusal on religious grounds, physical and mental fear of vaccinations or simply a stand of the basis of human rights. The reasons for refusal would be taken into account in determining the reasonableness or unreasonableness of the employer's response to the employee's refusal.

If an employer fails to implement the guidance and a client is infected by a health care professional, then the employer could face an action in negligence both for its direct liability and also for its vicarious liability for the negligence of its staff in course of employment.

The independent midwife
Whilst she is not obliged by a term in a contract of employment to accept the NHS Management Executive guidance, she does have a duty of care in the law of negligence to the client. If she infected a client with hepatitis B then she could face a claim against her. Her honorary contract with an NHS trust to use their premises for the delivery of her own clients may also include an expectation that the independent midwife complies with the NHS management executive guidance.

The local supervising authority
All midwives, whether employed or self employed, have a duty to follow the policies of the local supervising authority. The LSA has the power to suspend a midwife from practice when necessary for the purpose of preventing the spread of infection (Rule

38). Rule 39 requires a practising midwife to undergo medical examination if the LSA deem it necessary for preventing the spread of infection. Whilst the LSA is not the employer of the midwife, these powers could be used to supplement the NHS management executive guidance on the protection against hepatitis B.

One might query why any reasonable midwife who wants to ensure her own safety and that of her clients should contemplate refusing to follow guidance which is designed to safeguard both. However it is essential that there should be a review in depth of the arguments for and against compulsory protection and the legal basis for any enforcement. Just as 'Changing Childbirth' encourages mothers to have a greater say in their care during pregnancy, childbirth and after care, so midwives should ensure that they look critically at any instruction given to them which purports to protect their health and that of their clients and have a clear understanding of the legal issues involved.

Community care and the midwife

Midwives visit homes with extremes of conditions – from the wealthy with every facility and luxury to the very poor, with dangerous and dilapidated furnishings, fittings and even structure. Incidents could include:

- a community midwife falls down the stairs in the client's home as a result of a broken banister.
- the midwife catches her foot in a worn carpet and suffers severe injury to her arm.
- an accident occurs because the electric kettle is dangerous.

Activity | **Untimed activity**

Identify possible accidents which could occur in a home and analyse who is responsible for compensating the midwife for harm. This will include identifying the laws which apply.

Commentary
There are three possible sources of liability for the personal injury to the midwife:

- Her employer
- The occupier of the premises
- The owner of the premises (if that is different from the occupier).

The employer has a contractual duty to take reasonable care for the safety of the employee. This includes the provision of a safe system of work, safe plant equipment and premises and competent staff. If the midwife is able to show that she has suffered personal injury because of a failure by the employer to take reasonable care of her, then she could claim against him. Thus if she were injured on hospital premises because the equipment provided was not safe, the employer would be liable.

The difficulty in the community is that the employer is not responsible for the premises the midwife visits. If very dangerous conditions prevail, such as where the client or relative has threatened violence, then the employer should take reasonable care in such circumstances, perhaps by ensuring that the midwife was accompanied. If the midwife has to visit dangerous areas, the provision of alarms or two-way radios might be reasonably expected of the employer.

However where the injury is caused by the condition of the premises or its furnishings which are not in the control of the employer, the employer is not liable if the midwife should be injured.

The midwife therefore would have to look to the occupier or the owner of the property depending upon the responsibility for the cause of the accident. It could be that the accident was caused by failures of a landlord to maintain the structure of the building in a safe condition, or it could be failures of the occupier in relation to furniture and fittings which were his responsibility. The midwife would have a right of action under the Occupier's Liability Act 1957. However, unless the owner or occupier has insurance cover or is able to pay the costs personally, the midwife may have a legal right of action but no possibility of recovering the compensation. It is therefore advisable for a midwife to check whether she is covered for such personal accidents either by her own personal cover, or by her employer's insurance cover, or by cover from her professional association.

Health and safety, employment law and whistle blowing

You have seen from the textbook and from the exercise above that health and safety duties are integral to the contract of employment and the reciprocal duties of employer and employee. Recent changes in employment legislation have strengthened the position of the employee who is faced with a health and safety hazard and the employer appears reluctant to take action. Pages 186–87 of the textbook give details of new laws which protect the employee in certain health and safety situations. Note that the employee would be expected to work through the recognized channels of health and safety representatives and health and safety committees. Should she be dismissed in the circumstances set out on p. 187 the dismissal is automatically unfair.

Whistle blowing

Midwives may sometimes consider that a danger exists to their clients or colleagues but that management appears not to be taking appropriate action. Such a situation is sometimes described as a whistle blowing one, where the employee might consider that notifying the press is the only recourse. The government has issued guidance on relations with the press and media and advised each employer to establish a mechanism whereby any concerns of employees can be made known to higher levels of management without the individual fearing victimization.

> **Activity** — **2 hours**
>
> Obtain a copy of circular on Relations with the Press and Media (NHS Management Executive, 1993), Guidance for Staff on Relations with the Public and Media, circular EL(93)51) and a copy (if it exists) of your employer's grievance procedure drawn up in response to the circular.
>
> Imagine a situation where harm could occur to a client if action were not taken: it could be a case of inadequate resources, an unsafe system of work, a lack of training, or lack of good communications between professionals.
>
> List the action which you would take to improve the situation, writing down the evidence you would require to make out a rational case for change.
>
> - Assume that each level of management fails to act appropriately and you have to take the issue up with the next one. What further information and evidence would you require?
> - What is the final line of action which you could take? What laws apply?
> - To what extent have you observed the rules of confidentiality in pursuing your concerns?

Commentary

One would hope that in well-managed organizations you do not have to go far up the management hierarchy to secure effective action to resolve the situation. Where the midwife's immediate manager is a practitioner registered with the UKCC, she is able to point out that any failure of a registered practitioner as manager to meet concerns relating to health and safety matters could constitute professional misconduct by the manager who could face misconduct proceedings before the professional conduct committee.

Use this activity as a basis if in the future an actual problem arises of hazard to client or colleague where you find it difficult to get action.

Stress at work

The employer's duty to take reasonable care of the employee's health and safety also includes the duty to take reasonable care of the employee's mental well-being. In a recent case a social worker won a case brought against his employers when he was forced to take early retirement following a second work related breakdown.

The facts of the case were:

Mr John Walker had worked as an area social services officer with Northumberland County Council for 17 years. He was responsible for managing four teams of social services field workers in the Blyth Valley area of Northumberland, an area particularly productive of child care problems. In the 1980s he came under increasingly intense pressure as a population increase in the area led to a significant rise in child care cases. He frequently requested from his superiors further staff and management guidance but neither was forthcoming.

At the end of 1986 he suffered a nervous breakdown and under medical advice remained off work until March 1987. He had no previous history of mental disorder and it was common ground that his illness was attributable to the impact on his personality of his work. He returned to work but advised his superior that the pressure of his job had to be relieved. His superior agreed that an assistant would be available for as long as he was needed. The assistant, however, was only able to visit Mr Walker intermittently due to his own workload and after a month was unable to assist at all. Mr Walker was attempting to deal with a substantial backlog of paper work as well as an ever increasing number of child care cases.

In 1987 he suffered a second nervous breakdown and was obliged to retire from his post. As a consequence he was incapable of returning to his chosen career or of taking on work which involved the shouldering of significant responsibilities. In 1988 he was dismissed from his post on the ground of permanent ill health.

The basis of Mr Walker's claim for compensation was that the defendants owed a duty of care to provide a safe system of work, and it was in breach of this duty in as much as the system of work was a threat to mental health which remained unremedied and caused the plaintiff's breakdown.

The defendants agreed that a duty of care was owed to the plaintiff to exercise reasonable care to provide him with a reasonably safe working system and to protect him from risks which were reasonably foreseeable – it claimed that there had been no breach of that duty. Alternatively they argued that if the risk was reasonably foreseeable, the defendant did not act unreasonably in failing to relieve the pressure in all the circumstances and in particular the budgetary constraints of the social services department. The only effective remedial measures would have involved increasing staff by allocating additional funds and as applying the defendant's limited resources involved policy making as distinct from operational decisions, the defendant could not be said to have been in breach of any duty of care in having failed to take those decisions.

The judge accepted that on the facts Mr Walker's superior was aware that social service staff were operating on a crisis management basis, that they were understaffed and in urgent need of restructuring to relieve the pressure of work in the area. In addition the superior knew that the rapidly expanding demand for field services would make Mr Walker's management responsibilities increasingly difficult to carry out and that Mr Walker had a growing sense that nothing was being done at county level to alleviate the position.

WHAT WAS THE NATURE OF THE DUTY OWED BY THE EMPLOYER?

The judge in reviewing the authorities on the nature of the duty owed by employer to employee appreciated that most cases were concerned with physical injury. However, he stated that there was no logical reason why psychiatric damage should be excluded from the scope of the duty of care owed by the employer. Nor should psychiatric damage be excluded from the implied term in the contract of employment.

WAS THERE A BREACH OF THIS DUTY BY THE EMPLOYER?

What criteria were used to decide if there had been a breach? In determining the standard of care which should have been provided, the judge accepted that the practicability of remedial measures had clearly to take into account the resources and facilities at the disposal of the person or body owing the duty of care and the purpose of the activity which had given rise to the risk of injury.

The question was whether it ought to have been foreseen that the plaintiff was exposed to a risk of mental illness materially higher than that which would ordinarily affect a social services middle manager in his position with a really heavy workload.

The judge found that although the plaintiff's personality was normal, he had been driven to the point of despair by the defendant's failure to provide him with sufficient resources to satisfy urgent needs for the people in his area, thereby alleviate the work pressure. He had been trapped in a situation where on the one hand, he was unable to control the increasing volume of stressful work and where on the other, he was unable to persuade superior management to increase staff or give management guidance as to work distribution or prioritization.

The judge concluded that the first nervous breakdown might not have been reasonably foreseeable by the superior. However he was in no doubt that in the circumstances, the superior ought to have foreseen that if the plaintiff were once again exposed to the same workload, there was a risk that another breakdown would occur likely to end in a termination of his social services career.

The superior should have appreciated that the plaintiff was a man distinctly more vulnerable to psychiatric damage that he had appeared to be in 1986. The only course which would have had a reasonable probability of preventing another mental breakdown was the provision of continuous or substantial back up for the plaintiff.

The judge concluded that in the circumstances it would have been reasonable of the defendants to take action to alleviate or remove the risk of breakdown. In deciding what was reasonable conduct, regard had to be taken for the acute staffing and financial problems which confronted the defendant at the relevant time and of the fact and extent of disruption which would have been caused to other social work by assisting the plaintiff's area. The judge took the view that the dichotomy between a policy decision and an operational one, as argued by the defendants's barrister, had no more part to play in the context of the duty of care to an employee with whom a statutory body had an employment contract than it would have had in the context of any other contract made by such a body. There was no basis for treating a public body differently in principle from any other commercial employer, although considerations such as budget and inflexibility of decision-making might not arise with a commercial body.

His conclusions were:

> 'Having regard to the reasonably foreseeable size of risk of repetition of the plaintiff's illness and the reasonably foreseeable gravity of the breakdown which could have resulted if nothing were done to assist him, the standard of care to be expected of a reasonable local authority required that in March 1987 such additional assistance should have been provided if not on a permanent basis at least until restructuring of the social services had been effected and the work load on the plaintiff thereby permanently reduced.
>
> That additional assistance ought to have been provided notwithstanding that the defendant could have expected a disruptive effect on the provision of services to the public.'

WAS THERE CAUSATION?

There appeared to be no dispute that it was as a result of the effect of the situation at work upon Mr Walker's personality that the nervous breakdown was caused.

WAS THERE RECOGNIZABLE HARM?

As can be seen above the judge accepted that psychiatric harm could be compensated in the circumstances, as physical harm would have been.

HOW MUCH I.E WHAT WAS THE QUANTUM?

This amount payable by the defendants has been left to be agreed and was expected to be in the region of £200,000. The heads of damage would be the same as used in the calculation of physical harm. It would thus include pain and suffering, loss of income and future loss of earnings (see Chapter 12 of the textbook for calculation of quantum).

The implications of this case for midwives are clear. Note that the duty placed on the employer is only what is reasonable and it has to be reasonably foreseeable to the employer that the employee needs to have additional support. The midwife seeking to make a claim would have to establish clearly that in the particular circumstances of her work situation, the employer was in breach of this duty of care:

- they could reasonably foresee the risks of harm to the employee
- that there were reasonable measures which they failed to take
- that as a consequence of the failure the employee has suffered harm.

What is the significance of the specific weakness of an individual employee... a particular susceptibility?

In this case the judge did not find a breach of the duty of care in relation to the first breakdown, but the existence of this breakdown meant that the employers should have been aware of the employee's particular weaknesses. Thus if a midwife has had to take sick leave which has been brought on through stress in her work and she asks for reasonable help and support to be provided and on her return to work that assistance is not supplied, then should she become stressed again, there may be liability by the employer.

> **Activity** *Time taken for this activity will vary*
>
> A certain amount of stress at work is inevitable and may even be seen as a incentive. However there may come a point where it is not reasonable to expect an employee to take any more.
>
> Analyse your own work situation and the stresses which arise in it. Are any stresses reasonable? What action could you reasonably take to reduce those stresses? What action would it be reasonable for you to expect your employer to take?

Commentary
The employer has a general duty in relation to health and safety at work. This includes a duty in relation to mental health. The employer can be expected to take reasonable care of the mental health of the employee. Where the employee is known to have a particular susceptibility or weakness, then the burden on the employer is greater. It would probably be reasonable to expect the employee to be able to cope with a certain amount of stress. However it is likely that interviews could be more searching to check out a midwife's ability to cope with pressures of work. Midwives on their part must ensure that employers are aware when they are subject to unacceptable and unreasonable pressures, that documentation reflects the situation and that records are kept of the information which is passed to management and the action which is taken. This activity should have assisted you in drawing out the main elements which should be considered both by the employer and by the employee.

Another area of concern is the need for vigilance regarding the purchasing and maintenance of electrical and biomedical equipment. The Medical Devices Agency provides advice and guidance for employers and employees.

Health and safety in the future

Concern for health and safety issues can never be a once and for all matter. Every area of health and safety covered requires ongoing monitoring and review. One of the unfortunate aspects of health and safety is the rise and fall of 'topical' areas. At one moment there is concern about HIV/AIDS infection, then manual handling comes to the fore. Now as a result of the recent case brought by a social worker we are likely to see concern with stress. It is the responsibility of the midwife to attempt to ensure every area of significant risk is regularly monitored so that she ensures that she practices safely in relation to her client, her colleagues and herself.

Endnote

Health and safety law covers every aspect of accountability: liability in the civil and criminal courts, professional accountability before the UKCC and the relationship of employer and employee through the contract of employment. Before you move on to Section 8 covering care in the community and midwife managed units, check your understanding of health and safety laws by answering the following questions. Refresh your understanding by reading Chapters 18 and 28 again.

Self-assessment questions

- How is the Health and Safety Act 1974 and the regulations under it enforced?
- Name three terms implied into the contract of employment by the common law which relate to health and safety.
- How does the Code of Professional Conduct relate to health and safety laws?
- What is meant by the 6-pack regulations?
- What should the midwife do if she suspects that a mother is suffering from an infectious disease?

References

Dimond, B. (1994). *Legal Aspects of Midwifery*. Hale: Books for Midwives Press.
NHS Executive (1993). *Guidance EL(93)51*. London: HMSO.

SECTION EIGHT

The Midwife Working in the Community and Midwife Managed Units

This section enables you to identify and analyse:

- Legal perspectives of professional developments.
- Risk management strategies to reduce litigation.

This section includes an assessment opportunity. This could be suitable for AP(E)L assessment.

Alternatively this assessment may become the summative assessment for a distance learning module.

SECTION EIGHT

The Midwife Working in the Community and Midwife Managed Units

This section covers those specific topics which arise where the midwife is working in the community and also the legal problems which can emerge in the establishment and running of midwife managed units. Chapters 20 and 33 in the textbook are relevant.

Topics covered:

- The mother's right to give birth at home
- GPs and the midwife
- The obstetric services and the community midwife
- The midwife managed unit
- Health and safety in the community.

The mother's right to give birth at home

It will be remembered from unit three and the consideration of the 'Changing Childbirth' report that one of the aims was to give the mother a central role in the decision making relating to her confinement. One of the crucial decisions is the choice of place of birth. It is likely that there will be an increasing number of women who when given the choice would opt for a home confinement. There have been concerns expressed by midwives and GPs about professional responsibility and accountability related to intrapartum care. In December 1995 a joint statement from the Royal College of Midwives and the Royal College of General Practitioners clarified the roles of both midwives and GPs.

There will of course be situations where home birth is not clinically advisable and this could present the midwife with ethical and legal problems.

Activity — 15 minutes

There is no right to admit compulsorily the mother to hospital. List the advantages and disadvantages of a statute being passed to give the midwife the right to compel the mother to be admitted to hospital if it were necessary to save her life or that of the baby's.

Or

Activity

You are called, in an emergency, to the home of a woman who insists on giving birth at home. Whilst making the initial examination you note she has a lower abdominal scar. This was from a previous lower segment caesarean section one year ago.

List your concerns, your duty to the woman, and your professional responsibilities. What are the responsibilities of the GP and obstetrician in such a case if the woman chooses to remain at home?

Commentary

The joint working group reporting in the RCOG document Organizational Standards for Maternity Services (1995) give suggestions, for discussion at local level, on the specific standard and suggested method of audit for support for planned home delivery. The group state that,

> 'The standards recommended should be drafted with the acceptance of the principle that delivery in the mother's home, with appropriate selection of cases and attendants, is an acceptable practice in modern maternity care.' (p. 15)

The 'Changing Childbirth' report urges all health care personnel to collaborate with each other and work in partnership with the users of maternity services. Identify barriers to effective communication between GPs, obstetricians, midwives and mothers.

How can these be overcome in your area of work? Have difficulties in communication affected standards of care?

Activity — Untimed activity

Attend a meeting of your local Maternity Services Liaison committee (MSLC). Identify the membership and contact your midwife representative.

Choose one recommendation supported by the MSLC. Examine the recommendation from a legal perspective (using the main textbook and this workbook).

The Midwife Working in the Community and Midwife Managed Units

> **Activity** — **Untimed activity**
>
> Make out a report identifying the legal and professional codes that support or are compromised by the recommendations.
>
> Discuss these with the midwife representative on the MSLC.
>
> This activity could form the basis of an assessment of your ability to apply basic legal principles to a complex situation, providing recommendations within a legal framework.

Commentary
You may find the form in Appendix 3 of the workbook useful to assist your systematic review of any identified issues and professional concerns.

GPs and the midwife

It is essential that the midwife and the GP who has opted to provide maternity services develop a good relationship to ensure the welfare of the mother and baby.

> **Activity** — **Untimed activity**
>
> You are responsible for an antenatal clinic in a local GPs surgery. Whenever a woman opts for a home birth the GP 'off lists' the woman. Can the GP do this and still remain on the obstetric list approved by the Commissioning Authority?
>
> How can you overcome this recurrent problem and maintain a professional working relationship with the GP.

Commentary
Examine Appendix I and II in the textbook (pp. 311–16).

Read Davies and Young's *Report of the Association of Community Based Maternity Care's Study of the Results of the Northern Region's 1993 Home Birth Study* (ACBMC, 1995) and

Cronk, M. (1995). 'Are midwives prepared for the home birth challenge?'. *British Journal of Midwifery*, Vol. 3, No. 2, Feb, pp. 105–06.

The question of the appropriate training and education for GPs and midwives is under review. No health care professional can become complacent or disregard the need for continuing professional development. The UKCC has advice and rules regarding continuing professional development (UKCC, 1995).

Explore the possibility, with your colleagues, for an appropriate support and training programme for midwives (and GPs) who do not feel competent to care for a woman choosing a home birth.

Do doctors have similar requirements? What is the legal status of the refusal by the doctor refusing care? Is he in breach of his contract with the FHSA?

On July 19th 1995 it was announced that six GP practices would participate in piloting the purchasing of Maternity Services scheme. This initiative will be challenging the current patterns of maternity care provision in the six areas chosen (Partington, 1995 'GP fundholding – the assessment of purchasing maternity services'. *British Journal of Midwifery*, October, Vol. 3, No. 10, p. 561).

Evaluation of the pilot sites is planned over a two year period. Caroline Holland reports on one of the projects sites in an informative article published in *MIDIRS Midwifery Digest* (Vol.6, No.2, June 1996 pp. 130–132). Further exploration and discussion of the issues surrounding GP fundholding and purchasing maternity services has been written by Tyler (1996) in the *British Journal of Midwifery*, Vol.4, No.8, pp. 431–43.

Make a note to follow progress and note if any published reports highlight any contractual, professional and legal issues. One such issue is the debate surrounding the involvement of practice nurses in midwifery care. The legal implications and the problems related to job demarcation are examined by Professor Dimond in *Modern Midwife* (Vol. 6, No. 1, January 1996 pp.34–35). The UKCC Council Position Statement on Practice Nurses and Antenatal Care (Annexe 1 to Registrar's Letter 8/1996) supports the midwife's role in the provision of antenatal care, but also opens up the possibility for the development of local protocols and policies clarifying the contribution of the practice nurse.

The relationship between the midwifery services and the medical practitioners is crucial to responsive and effective provision of care. This symbiotic relationship needs to be fostered so that women are assured the care they receive is appropriate, and responsive to their individual needs.

Activity 4 hours

Listed are some of the activities which could assist you in preparing yourself and colleagues for providing midwifery led care.

1. Critically examine the referral criteria developed by the Chelsea and Westminster Healthcare Trust (Lewis, [1995] *MIDIRS Midwifery Digest*, Vol. 5, No. 2, June pp. 219–223).

Do you have similar criteria for referral to the medical practitioner? Do such protocols have any legal status?

The Midwife Working in the Community and Midwife Managed Units

> 2. What if the woman refuses your advice to be examined by a medical practitioner?
>
> - List the records and actions you should make in these circumstances.
> - Discuss with your clinical specialist or supervisor of midwives the support networks existing.
> - Are *you* able to take a detailed medical history thus enabling you to identify those women who would benefit from direct referral to the GP/obstetrician.
> - Have you the right to details of previous medical notes in the GPs surgery to help you make these decisions?
> - Do you have direct referral rights to appropriate medical, obstetric and paediatric services?
>
> 3. Do you have a standard complaints procedure. Who will deal with the oral and/or written complaints?

Commentary

Read again Chapter 33 in the textbook. This chapter highlights the concerns expressed by midwives when preparing to provide care in a 'stand alone' (not attached to a District General Hospital) midwifery led unit.

Examine offprint on 'Midwifery-managed units' (p. 116 of this workbook) and note the type of concerns highlighted by the midwives.

To implement any new pattern of care requires adjustments from all parties concerned. The medical profession has expressed concerns as well as support for the recommendations of 'Changing Childbirth' (1993) and other regional initiatives such as the recommendations of the Welsh Health Planning Forum (1991).

Consider the concerns expressed by medical colleagues (Cheyne et al, [1995] 'Working alongside a midwife-led care unit: what do obstetricians think?'. *British Journal of Obstetrics and Gynaecology,* June, Vol.102, pp. 485–87).

Read Chapter 10 in the main textbook and check that you would know the locally agreed procedure for dealing with a complaint from a client or her family.

Should you decide to develop a complaints procedure for a midwifery led service you should obtain a copy of 'Being Heard' (D016/BH/2M HSSH J06 3055 June 1994) the report of the review committee on NHS complaints procedures (Chaired by Prof. Alan Wilson). This report can be obtained from:

Forge Court
Reading Road,
Yateley,
Camberley,
Surrey GU17 7RX

Legal Aspects of Midwifery Workbook

GP fundholders

From Chapter 20 you will understand the changes which have taken place as a result of introducing into the NHS the concept of the internal market. One of the purchasers are now GP fundholders. Initially they were able to purchase from a limited list of health services. Then community services were added but they were not able to employ their own community health professionals. There are now pilot schemes exploring the complex issues surrounding GP fundholders being able to employ midwives and purchase midwifery care for their clients.

Draw on the previous examples and activities to assist you do the next activity.

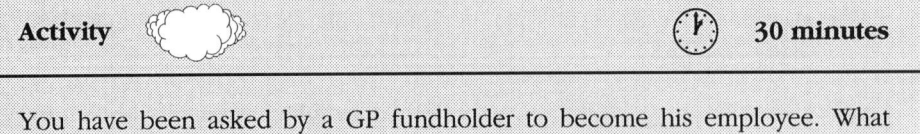

Activity   30 minutes

You have been asked by a GP fundholder to become his employee. What would be the benefits of this – for the mother, for the GP, for yourself? What conditions would you wish to see agreed in the contract of employment?

Commentary

This may seem an academic exercise at present but total fundholding could lead to the employment of midwives by GPs. If you can, check your answers to this exercise with the personnel officer of your Trust or with your shopsteward.

The obstetric services and the community midwife

It is essential that the midwife has an excellent relationship with the obstetric services.

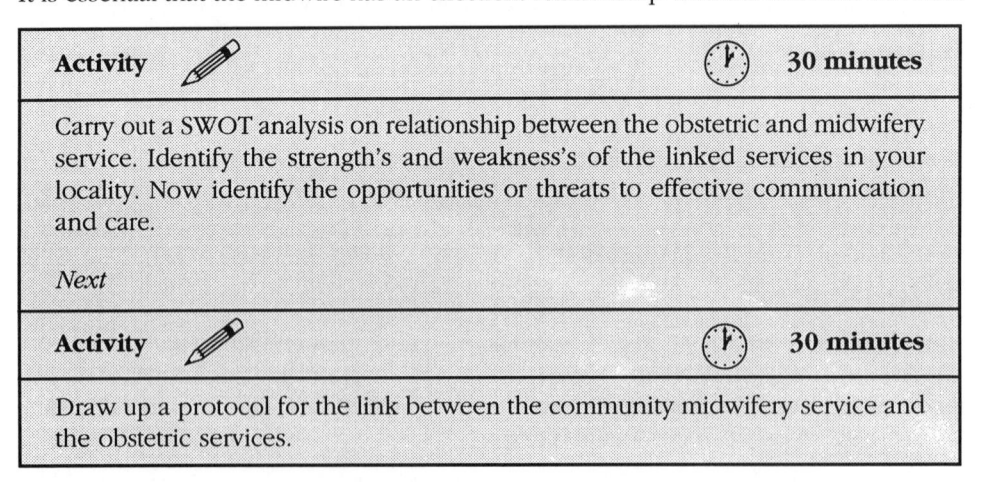

Activity   30 minutes

Carry out a SWOT analysis on relationship between the obstetric and midwifery service. Identify the strength's and weakness's of the linked services in your locality. Now identify the opportunities or threats to effective communication and care.

Next

Activity   30 minutes

Draw up a protocol for the link between the community midwifery service and the obstetric services.

Commentary

Both the above exercises should ensure a practical evaluation of the services in your area. Follow up your results with discussion with managers and colleagues on the bringing about of improvements.

The midwife managed unit

From Chapter 33 you will read of a risk assessment exercise which was carried out before a midwife managed unit was established. It is essential to have clear criteria for defining which mothers are appropriate for such an admission.

> **Activity** — **90 minutes**
>
> Draw up a check list for deciding if it were in the best interests of the mother and baby for a mother to have a home confinement or confinement in a midwife managed unit.
>
> Then identify all reasonable foreseeable risks of what could go wrong and work out what precautions could reasonably be taken in advance to minimize those risks. If necessary turn again to Section 7 on health and safety and refresh your memory on carrying out a risk assessment.

Commentary

Check your results with colleagues who work in such a unit or in the community and ascertain whether you have omitted from your list, risks of which they are aware.

Remember that if a mother *demands* admission to a midwife led unit (without obstetric/medical cover) the supervisor of midwives and the midwives providing care should have carefully prepared criteria for admission to the unit to which they can refer. Should a woman present with an obstetric or medical history requiring medical intervention, therefore beyond the scope of normal midwifery practice, the midwife *should* decline to meet the woman's demand. The midwife should advise the woman that her *needs* will be best met in an obstetric consultant unit. Mothers *do not* have a right to insist on admission to a midwife led unit contrary to a midwife's advice.

Health and safety in the community

The community midwife has very different health and safety problems compared with the hospital based midwife.

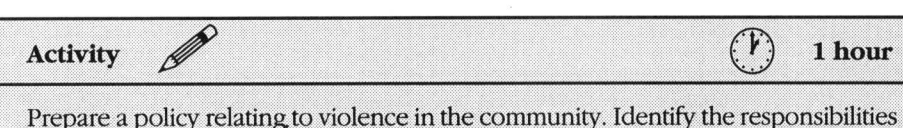

> **Activity** — **1 hour**
>
> Prepare a policy relating to violence in the community. Identify the responsibilities of the midwife and the responsibilities of the employer to ensure that the midwife is protected.

Legal Aspects of Midwifery Workbook

> **Activity** ✏️   🕐 **2 hours**
>
> Obtain a copy of the NHS Executive manual 'Risk management in the NHS' (D026/RISK/3M). This publication is free to the NHS from:
>
> BAPS
> HPU,
> DSS Distribution Centre, Heywood Stores,
> Manchester Road,
> Heywood,
> Lancashire, OL10 2PZ
>
> Read Chapter 11 on 'Identification of security risks' in the above named manual.
>
> - Reflect upon your own area of practice and/or that of the staff for whom you are managerially responsible.
> - Do you always leave a diary of proposed visits at your base so that your movements are known?
> - How would you contact a member of staff who has not reported to base when her rostered duty has finished?
> - If midwives are working flexible hours, to meet the needs of the clients how do the other members of the team know their whereabouts?
> - When working from home, especially if 'on call', how would your family and colleagues know where and by whom you had been called out to visit?
> - Who is responsible for the provision of effective communication systems?
> - Do you *always* use your identification badge when visiting premises in the course of your duty?
> - If a member of the public wished to verify your authenticity who would be immediately available to confirm that your visit was legitimate?

Commentary
Providing maternity care within hospital and community can never be totally safe. The risks to the individual can be reduced if all members of staff are conversant with their personal and professional role in the identification and management of risk assessment related to the provision of care.

Refer to Chapter 17 page 71 of the manual (risk management in the NHS). This section on personal safety will provide you with an insight into some of the issues which concern providers of community based care.

Remember that modern telephone communications systems provide the user with storing caller telephone numbers and tracing facilities. Using answer phones will also provide a record of those incoming messages so that your whereabouts could be more easily monitored.

Assessment opportunity
(Suitable for assessment at level 3)
- Using the principles of risk management prepare a checklist for midwives which will enable them to identify those issues and potential dangers to personal and clients safety.
- Evaluate the responses to the checklist and develop protocols to reduce risk to clients and staff.
- Prepare a programme of training and education for colleagues and other staff related to the locally identified needs.
- Keep a record of this exercise and the outcomes for your Personal Professional Profile.

Endnote
Even though you may expect to work mainly in a hospital context you need to have an understanding of the relationships and duties which arise in community care and midwife managed units. This is particularly important since the report on 'Changing Childbirth' and the emphasis on enabling women to choose the place of birth.

Check through the Chapter 5 (on 'Changing Childbirth') and 33 on midwifery managed units in the textbook and answer the following questions before you proceed with the next section on medication.

Self-assessment questions

- Can the midwife force the mother to be admitted to a district general hospital for the confinement?
- What does the midwife do if a husband or cohabitee insists upon being present at a home birth and interferes with the delivery?
- How do you enforce the agreed criteria for the use of a midwife managed unit in relation to mothers and GPs?
- What responsibilities does the GP have if he has accepted the mother for maternity services?
- What conditions should be seen as never enabling the mother to have a home confinement or confinement in a midwife managed unit?

References
Cheyne, H. et al. (1995). 'Working alongside a midwifery led care unit'. *British Journal of Obstetrics and Gynaecology*, Vol.102, No.6, pp.485–87.
Cronk, M. (1995). 'Are midwives prepared for the homebirth challenge?'. *British Journal of Midwifery*, Vol.3, No.2, pp.105–106.
Davies, J., Young, G. (1993). *Report of the Association of Community based Maternity Care: Study of Northern region Homebirth study*. ACBMC.
Department of Health (1994). *Being Heard: The Report of a Review Committee on NHS Complaints Procedures*. London: HMSO.
Dimond, B. (1994). *Legal Aspects of Midwifery*. Hale: Books for Midwives Press.

Dimond, B. (1994). 'Midwifery-managed units'. *Modern Midwife*, Vol.4, No.6, pp.31–33.
Dimond, B. (1996). *Modern Midwife*. Vol.6, No.1, pp.34–35.
Holland, C. (1996). 'GP fundholding how does it affect midwives'. *MIDIRS Midwifery Digest* Vol.6, No.2, pp.130–132.
Lewis, P. (1995). 'Refining the model – group practice midwifery'. *MIDIRS Midwifery Digest* Vol.5, No.2, pp.219–223.
NHS Executive (1995). *Risk Management in NHS*. London: HMSO.
Partington, K. (1995). 'GP fundholding'. *British Journal of Midwifery*. Vol.3, No.10, p.561.
Royal College of Midwives, Royal College of General Practitioners (1995). *Joint Statement*. London: RCM, RCGP.
Royal College of Obstetricians and Gynaecologists (1995). *Organisational Standards for Maternity Services*. London: RCOG.
Tyler, S. (1996). 'Making GP fundholding work for midwives'. *British Journal of Midwifery* Vol.4, No.8, pp.431–43.
UKCC (1995). *PREP and You*. London: UKCC.
UKCC (1996). *Registrar's Letter 8/96 Annexe 1*. London: UKCC.
Welsh Health Planning Forum (1991). *Protocol for Investment in Health Gain: Maternal and Early Child Health*. Welsh Office: HMSO.

SECTION NINE

The Legal Aspects of Medication

On completion of this section you should be able to provide evidence of:

- Your understanding of the legislative framework related to midwives prescribing.

- Your ability to identify risks and develop risk reduction strategies in all care environments.

SECTION NINE

The Legal Aspects of Medication

Midwives have had greater powers given to them by law than other practitioners registered with the UKCC in the prescribing of medications. Even when nurse prescribing is implemented across the whole country it is likely that the midwife will still be in an exceptional situation in relation to medication. Chapter 19 of the textbook should be read through together with the relevant sections of the Midwives Rules and the Midwives Code of Practice and also the UKCC publications on Standards for the Administration of Medicines (1992) and UKCC Guidelines for Professional Practice (1996).

This section seeks to give to the midwife an understanding of the legal issues given below:

- The legislative framework
- The Rules and UKCC guidance on the administration of medicines
- Standards for administering and prescribing
- Record keeping and medicines
- The mother as a drug addict.

The legislative framework

The different categories of medicines are set out in the Medicines Act 1968. Different regulations apply to the different categories. A pharmacist has recently faced a hearing before the pharmaceutical committee of the FHSA for failure to dispense prescription only drugs against the prescription. Because the drugs were cheaper than the prescription charge he sold the drugs to the patient at the actual price. The midwife should obtain copies of any procedures, practices and protocols drawn up by her employer in relation to the handling of the different medicinal products.

Activity	2 hours
Draw up a protocol for administering controlled drugs, distinguishing between the different schedules of controlled drugs and also drawing a distinction between the role of the midwife in the community and the midwife in the hospital context.	

The Legal Aspects of Medication

Commentary
When undertaking the above activity you need to have considered the role of the medical practitioner and pharmacist along with the role and responsibilities of the midwife.

The UKCC advisory document 'Scope of Professional Practice' (1992) and the 'Standards for the Administration of Medicines' (1992) provide guidance.

> Study offprints 'Medication and the midwife: statutory control' and 'The midwife's power to prescribe' (pp.121-127 of this workbook).

Revise Chapter 19 in the textbook, reflect upon your personal practice. The practical interpretation of the role of the midwife and the legislation and regulations surrounding this role are outlined and discussed in series of articles by Simpson and Smith published in the *British Journal of Midwifery* (Simpson, D., Smith, R. [1995]. 'Drugs, the law and the midwife: 1'. *British Journal of Midwifery*, August, Vol. 3., No. 8.; Simpson, D., Smith, R. [1995]. 'Drugs, law and the midwife: 2'. *British Journal of Midwifery*, October Vol.3, No.10).

The Rules and UKCC guidance on the administration of medicines

Rule 41 relating to the administration of drugs is set out on page 192 Table 19.2. This is amplified in the Midwife's Code of Practice (paragraphs 24–27 Table 19.4 of the textbook p.193). Additional procedures need to be drawn up to cover some of the situations which the midwife is likely to encounter in the administration of medicines.

Activity — **Timing for this activity will vary**

Do a brain storming session, preferably with a midwife colleague, or if necessary on your own, on the foreseeable risks which could arise in the administration of drugs in the community and in the hospital. Then identify measures which could be taken to reduce the chance of these risks arising.

Commentary
When identifying risks remember to refer to the NHS Management manual *Risk Management in the NHS* (as mentioned in Section 8 of the workbook). Use the suggested format (Chapter 3, p. 9 'Risk identification and analysis techniques').

Legal Aspects of Midwifery Workbook

Standards for administering and prescribing

Supplement the material cited in the above subsection with the guidance from the UKCC on standards for the administration of medicines.

Activity **Time taken for this activity will vary**

Case study

Mary has been a practising community based midwife for the past ten years. She has recently started to provide midwifery led care to women in the community and hospital setting. One of the women Mary is providing care for, Jane, requested a home birth. This was contrary to Mary's advice (the previous birth was assisted by the use of Ventouse vacuum extraction. Jane stated this was because of a delay in the second stage of labour causing fetal distress).

Following a long and painful labour the decision was made that this birth should occur in the local maternity unit where an anaesthetist would be available to provide the woman with regional anaesthesia by means of an epidural cannulation.

The woman and her partner agreed to transfer to the hospital and expected Mary to continue to provide care. The epidural cannula was inserted successfully by the anaesthetist and Mary assisted in this procedure. The woman needed further 'top-up' to the epidural and Mary decided to administer the local anaesthetic through the cannula. Mary continued to provide care throughout the night as the labour ward was unusually busy that night. The woman subsequently gave birth to a live baby again assisted by the use of a Ventouse extraction. Following the birth mother and baby appeared fine.

Two years later Jane is told her baby has brain damage. In addition to this Jane has had a history of severe back pain since the last birth. The medication which Mary had administered via the epidural cannula has now become subject to questioning and civil and criminal action is being mentioned. The incident has been reported to the UKCC and Mary's employer's have asked her to attend for disciplinary proceedings.

Identify how the four different areas of accountability are likely to proceed. What records and evidence would Mary require to show that she was not at fault?

You may find the form (Appendix 3 in this workbook) developed to systematically evaluate an incident, a useful starting point in this activity.

The Legal Aspects of Medication

Commentary
This case study highlights the need for proactive midwifery supervision. If Mary had taken the opportunity to explore her personal professional needs (see Appendix 4 in this workbook) with her supervisor of midwives, then the outcome of this case may have been different.

Finally the importance of record keeping and taking responsibility for ones own professional development are highlighted.

Record keeping and medicines
Revise the guidance issued by the UKCC and also the paragraphs in the Rules which relate to record keeping and medication.

Activity	Untimed activity
Scrutinize the records relating to medication over the past three months and see if you can identify any errors in record keeping. How well would the records stand up to any civil action in which they were required as direct evidence?	

The mother as a drug addict
The illegal use of a variety of substances is not confined to a distinct group of users. Midwives need to be aware that some women they provide care for may well be habitual or 'recreational' users of any variety or combination of 'street' drugs. Women using drugs in this way may choose not to tell their midwife. This could present you with difficulties when offering a choice of analgesia during labour. Some NHS Trusts have well developed services to support the pregnant drug addict.

Activity	Timing for this activity will vary
Find out the extent of drug related problems in your area. Develop links with any local iniatives involving midwives, arrange a visit to discuss the midwife's role. What action should the midwife take if she discovers that one of her mothers is addicted to drugs? Use the form in Appendix 3 to assist your systematic review.	

Commentary
This area of practice is not just confined to midwives practicing in inner city areas. Midwives have a responsibility to develop insight and understanding of the local extent of the problem thus enabling the midwife to provide appropriately targeted care. Further information can be gained from the following source: Siney, C. (1995). *The Pregnant Drug Addict.* Hale, Cheshire: Books for Midwives Press.

Legal Aspects of Midwifery Workbook

Endnote

This is an extremely important area of practice for the midwife and she must be confident in her understanding of the relevant law. Answer the following questions and reread Chapter 19 and the recommended UKCC publications before you proceed to Section 10 which covers specific areas of law relating to midwifery practice.

Self-assessment questions:

- State two Acts of Parliament which set the framework for the control of medicines.
- What is meant by controlled drugs and identify the categories?
- What duties does the midwife have in relation to the supply of medicines?
- What Rules relate to the disposal of drugs?
- What effect will changes in the Nurse Prescribing laws have on the midwife?

References

Dimond, B. (1994). *Legal Aspects of Midwifery*. Hale: Books for Midwives Press.
Dimond, B. (1994). 'Medication and the midwife: statutory control'. *Modern Midwife*, Vol.4, No. 10, pp.34–35.
Dimond, B. (1994). 'The midwife's power to practice'. *Modern Midwife*, Vol.4, No.11, pp.34–35.
NHS Executive (1995). *Risk Management in the NHS*. London: HMSO.
Simpson, D., Smith, R. (1995). 'Drugs, the law and the midwife: 1'. *British Journal of Midwifery*, Vol.3, No.8.
Simpson, D., Smith, R. (1995) 'Drugs, the law and the midwife: 2'. *British Journal of Midwifery*, Vol.3, No.10.
Siney, C. (1995). *The Pregnant Drug Addict*. Hale: Books for Midwives Press.
UKCC (1992). *Standards for the Administration of Medicines*. London: UKCC.
UKCC (1993). *Midwives Rules*. London: UKCC.
UKCC (1994). *The Midwife's Code of Practice*. London: UKCC.
UKCC (1996). *Guidelines for Professional Practice*. London: UKCC.

SECTION TEN

Specific Areas of Law

> In this section you have the opportunity to state your own objectives.
>
> However, it is recommended that you study and review your practice related to statutory provisions in childbirth and death.

SECTION TEN

Specific Areas of Law

In this final section we cover some of the more specialist areas of law. Time does not permit, in the estimated hours laid down for this module, for all the different areas to be covered. It is therefore suggested that you should undertake the first subsection of this section and then choose one of the remaining topics to cover. If you are able to invest more time in the study, you could undertake as many additional areas as you wish.

The following areas are covered:

- Statutory provisions in childbirth and death (it is recommended that you should study this area).

Choose one from the following:

- Human Fertilization and Embryology Act and subsequent developments
- The status of the fetus and Abortion Act 1967 (as amended)
- Children Act 1989
- Legal issues in teaching and research.

Statutory provisions in childbirth and death

This subsection covers:

- procedures following birth of child
- death of child
- stillbirth
- registration and certification
- use of fetal material
- supporting the parents
- the status and rights of the fetus.

Chapters 24 and 16 of the textbook cover this area.

Specific Areas of Law

Activity	4 hours
Study Chapter 24 of the textbook and then draw up a leaflet for mothers and midwives setting out the duties set by Act of Parliament in relation to a birth, still birth or birth and death. If possible see if you can visit the local registrars office and collect specimens of the forms, which are kept there. Ensure that your leaflet highlights the different laws relating to the disposal of the body.	

Commentary
It is essential that the midwife is familiar with the rules relating to registration and certification of birth and death, since she needs to give to the mother confident and accurate advice at this emotional time.

Still birth

As you will have seen from the text a fetus born after 24 weeks gestation which does not breathe or show any signs of life is defined as 'still born'. It must be registered as such. Even where the pregnancy has not lasted into the 24th week, the mother and father and family need support. The bereavement and grieving process can result in long term problems and as such midwives should be knowledgable about the legal requirements so that these can be dealt with sensitively and promptly, whilst meeting the individual family's needs. A moving account of one couples sensitive and appropriate care can be found in SAFTA News, November 1995, pp. 4–6.

Activity	2 hours
Prepare a policy for assisting parents in coping with still birth or miscarriage before 24 weeks or neonatal death.	
Discuss the implications for midwives with colleagues and ensure that your policy takes into account the need to ensure support for midwives in handling such situations.	

Commentary
Obtain a copy of the current local policy/protocol related to the management of still birth and neonatal death. Compare this with the specific standard suggested in the RCOG report of a joint working group on Organizational Standards for Maternity Services (1995). Does the local protocol/policy meet with the recommendations set out. What audit mechanisms are in place locally?

Legal Aspects of Midwifery Workbook

Status and rights of the fetus

From Chapter 16 you will see that the law protects the fetus by specific offences which make it a criminal offence to cause a miscarriage. The Abortion Act 1967 (as amended) provides a defence to this Act in specific circumstances. This is considered below. The law does not, however, recognize the fetus as a legal personality capable of bringing an action, until it is born. In the case of Re S a woman was compelled to have a caesarean operation against her will to protect her life and that of the fetus. However as you will see from the RCOG guidelines (these are set out in more detail in Chapter 6, Table 6.8), there is disapproval of the decision.

The statute which gives compensation for prenatal negligence to the fetus, once born alive, is the Congenital Disabilities Act 1976 (see pp. 165–67 and pp. –317–19). Note the additional sections which have been added by the Human Fertilization and Embryology Act 1990 which are shown below in the section covering that Act.

Activity ✎   ⏲ **30 minutes**

In the light of the Congenital Disabilities Act 1976 answer the question whether the child, once born, could succeed in an action for negligence under the Act in the following circumstances:

- The child is born suffering from disabilities as a result of the mother being addicted to illegal drugs when pregnant.
- The father was suffering from a sexually transmitted disease at the time of conception. When the baby was born tests revealed that the baby had syphilis. The mother was not aware of the situation.
- The mother has agreed to an amniocentesis to determine if the fetus has Down's syndrome. Owing to negligence in the laboratory which analysed the sample, the fact that the fetus has Down's syndrome was not discovered.
- The pregnant mother is injured when she falls down stairs in a neighbours house as a result of a floor board giving way. The baby is born prematurely and suffers severe disabilities because of the injury to the mother.
- The mother consents to treatment from a hypnotist when pregnant and in this hypnotic trance falls off a stage.
- The mother is given an anti-emetic drug when pregnant, as a result of which the child is born with shortened limbs.
- A pregnant woman is driving a car whilst under the influence of alcohol and crashes it onto an oncoming vehicle. The baby is born with disabilities as a result of the crash.

Commentary

a) There is no right for the child to bring an action under the Congenital Disabilities Act against the mother because she was taking drugs during the pregnancy and has thereby harmed the fetus. The only circumstances in which the mother can be sued is if she was driving a car (see g. below). There is no right of action at common law, since the 1976 Act replaces the common law situation. There may be a possibility of suing a supplier of drugs, or manufacturer of drugs, under the Consumer Protection Act 1987, but any defence which could have been raised against the mother, were she to have sued them, could be raised against the child.

b) If the father were aware of the fact that he was suffering from VD and as a result has caused harm to the child, he could be liable under 1 (3). Under 1 (4) if the child's father knew of the prenatal risk of the child being born disabled, and the mother did not, the father could be liable. The question does not state whether the mother knew he had VD. If she did the child does not have a right of action.

c) The mother clearly has a case against the employers of the laboratory technician for failure to analyse the sample appropriately. However, the child's disabilities are not the result of this negligence. The child's cause of action is that it has been born at all, since a careful testing would probably lead to an abortion. It was established in the case of McKay v. Essex HA (1982) that the child does not have an action for wrongful life.

d) The occupier is at fault in failing to take reasonable care to ensure that a visitor would be reasonably safe for the purposes for which he or she is invited onto the premises. Here there is a prima facie of a breach by the occupier of duties under the Occupier's Liability Act 1957. Since the child was born disabled as a result of this tort against the mother, she\he has the right of action under the Congenital Disabilities Act 1976.

e) The hypnotist owes a duty of care to the mother. If it can be established that he is in breach of this duty, then the child can bring an action under the Congenital Disabilities Act 1976. Any defence available against the mother can be used against the child, but if the hypnotist attempted to exempt himself from any liability, this exemption would not be effective as a result of the Unfair Contract Terms Act 1977, which prevents the exclusion of liability where personal injury or death result from negligence.

f) This situation is comparable to the thalidomide disaster, though the manufacturers Distillers, were never sued successfully in this country. The child has a prima facie case under the 1976 Act but would have to show that there was fault by the manufacturers. Alternatively an action might lie under the Consumer Protection Act 1987. In such an action it would have to be established that there was a defect in the product, judged accordingly to the state of knowledge at the time of manufacture.

Legal Aspects of Midwifery Workbook

g) The only situation under the 1976 Act where the mother can be sued by the child is where she is negligent whilst driving a car, and as a result caused harm to the fetus so that he/she was born disabled. The reason is that in practice the child would be seeking to obtain compensation from the insurers. In other situations, such as where the mother was smoking, drinking or taking drugs and thereby harmed the child, there would not necessarily be any funds which the child could claim against, and therefore giving a child a legal cause of action would not be conducive to family harmony.

Human Fertilization and Embryology Act 1990 and issues relating to contraception

Midwives may well be caring for a pregnancy which is the result of in vitro fertilization or they may be told that the mother is intending that the baby should be passed over to a man and woman who provided the gametes and she is therefore a surrogate mother.

Chapter 26 of the textbook covers this topic.

The Congenital Disabilities (Civil Liability) Act 1976 has been amended to take account of the possibility of congenital disabilities arising from IVF or artificial insemination.

The additional section 1A is shown below.

The Congenital Disabilities (Civil Liability) Act 1976 1A (1). In any case where:

- a child carried by a woman as the result of the placing in her of an embryo or of sperm and eggs or her artificial insemination is born disabled,
- the disability results from an act or omission in the course of the selection, or the keeping or use outside the body, of the embryo carried by her or of the gametes used to bring about the creation of the embryo, and
- a person is under this section answerable to the child in respect of the act or omission, the child's disabilities are to be regarded as damage resulting from the wrongful act of that person and actionable accordingly at the suit of the child.

(2) Subject to subsection (3) below and the applied provisions of section 1 of this Act, a person (here referred to as the 'defendant') is answerable to the child if he was liable in tort to one or both the parents (here referred to as 'the parent or parents concerned') or would, if sued in due time, have been so; and it is no answer that there could not have been such liability because the parent or parents concerned suffered no actionable injury, if there was a breach of legal duty which, accompanied by injury, would have given rise to the liability.

(3) The defendant is not under this section answerable to the child if at the time the embryo, or the sperm and eggs, are placed in the woman or the time of her insemination, (as the case may be) either or both of the parents knew the risk of their child being born disabled (that is to say the particular risk created by the act or omission).

Specific Areas of Law

(4) Subsection (5) to (7) of section 1 of this Act apply for the purposes of this selection as they apply for the purposes of that but as if references to the parent or the parent affected were references to the parent or parents concerned.

Additional section 4A:
In any case where a child carried by a woman as the result of the placing in her of an embryo or of sperm and eggs or her artificial insemination is born disabled, any reference in section 1 of this Act to a parent includes a reference to a person who would be a parent but for sections 27 to 29 of the Human Fertilization and Embryology Act 1990. (Sections 27-29 cover the definition of mother and father – see pages 249–50 and Tables 26.5 and 26.6.)

Activity **Untimed activity**

Study the following case study and answer the questions in the light of the Human Fertilization and Embryology Act 1990 and the Congenital Disabilities (Civil Liability) Act 1976 as amended. Also refer for more detail to the textbook on the Human Fertilization Act 1990 by Derek Morgan and Robert G (1991).

Julie and Bruce had been married for 12 years and were desperate to have children. Following medical examination it was established that Julie would never be able to bear a child, but she could produce eggs. She and Bruce therefore agreed that they would have a surrogacy arrangement whereby Emily, an unmarried mother, would have the embryo formed from Julie's egg fertilized by Bruce's sperm inserted in her. It was agreed that Bruce and Julie would pay all Emily's expenses. In addition there was a secret contract that Emily would be paid £10,000 when the baby was handed over.

During the pregnancy Emily became uncertain as to whether she wished to hand the baby over to the genetic parents. Julie visited her in hospital at the confinement and brought £10,000 in cash which Emily accepted because she had lots of debts. Subsequently when Julie and Bruce applied for a section 30 order from the court allowing then to adopt the baby, Emily stated that she would fight them all the way and refused to agree to any handover.

- What is the legal situation?
- Can Emily prevent the adoption?
- Will the £10,000 be refundable?
- What rights do the genetic parents have?
- Could Emily's mother apply to adopt the child?
- If Emily disagreed to the handover and then it was discovered that the baby suffered from an inherited disease, could she compel Julie and Bruce to adopt the child?
- If it is discovered that as a result of negligence by the technician in the laboratory, the embryo was damaged and is now suffering from severe disabilities, what right of action does the disabled child have?

Commentary

The Act tried to anticipate most of these issues which were initially considered by the Warnock Committee. If possible attempt to obtain a copy of the Warnock report and read the main recommendations and the minority report and you will understand the difficult issues and conflicts which had to be confronted.

> By reading the two offprints 'In vitro fertilization and the law' and 'The scope of fertility treatment' (pp. 128–134 of this workbook), you will be introduced to the complexity of this issue.

The status of the fetus and Abortion Act 1967 (as amended)
See Chapter 25 of the textbook.

Midwives are sometimes asked to assist on gynaecology wards and assist in the termination of pregnancies. Those midwives who cannot accept this work on grounds of conscience should read the statutory provisions relating to conscientious objection set out on page 242. Note that the defence does not apply when treatment is necessary to save the life or prevent grave permanent injury to the physical or mental health of a pregnant woman (see p. 0244).

Activity — 30 minutes

After studying Chapter 25 consider the legality of the following situations. In each case identify the section and subsection, if any which applies to the situation:

- An unmarried mother with three children seeks an abortion on the grounds that she would lose her job.
- Following amniocentesis, a pregnant woman is told that the fetus is Down's Syndrome.
- Following amniocentesis, a pregnant woman is told that the fetus has a 80 per cent probability of being dyslexic (assuming that a genetic screening test for this condition is eventually discovered).

Commentary

This activity should not have caused difficulties because of the clear wording of each subsection. Note however that the 24 week time limit only applies to the first subsection. There is no time limit for the remaining subsection, though abortions after 24 weeks are extremely rare.

Children Act 1989

Midwives may have concerns relating to the protection of existing children of mothers or the safety and health of the expected child. Chapter 31 sets out the main provisions of the Children Act 1989.

Specific Areas of Law

> **Activity** 2 hours
>
> Read Chapter 31 in the textbook and obtain your local policy covering child protection. Read the guidance issued by the Department of Health on child protection.
>
> Now check that you are able to name the local senior midwife/clinical specialist responsibilities for child protection and in service training related to the Children Act 1989.
>
> - Identify those persons to whom you should report any suspected abuse.
> - Would you report this in writing or verbally?
> - Are there incident forms available for you to record the concerns?
> - Who makes the decision to carry out further investigations?
> - Should there be any conflict regarding confidentiality?
> - What other agencies are involved with protecting the interest of children?
> - What would you do if you were confronted with a suspected case of child abuse in the family you were visiting?
> - What records would you make?
> - Would these be in the client held records?
> - Who can obtain access to the records?
>
> 1 hour
>
> Finally draw up a checklist for midwives and a 'flow chart' showing the approved referral route in cases of suspected abuse.

Commentary

If there were any of these questions which you could not answer, you should follow this up with a senior manager or a member of the Area Child Protection Committee. Make sure you have the up to date policy, since the re-establishment of new unitary authorities has led to new policies and new committees in some areas.

Legal issues in teaching and research

Chapters 29 and 30 deal with the legal situations which are likely to arise in teaching and research. Revise earlier chapters covering areas such as consent and confidentiality and negligent misstatements which are also the concern of the teacher and researcher.

> **Activity** 30 minutes
>
> It is essential that the liability for the midwifery tutor is clarified when she is undertaking clinical supervision of her students in an NHS trust.

Legal Aspects of Midwifery Workbook

> Obtain from your employers a copy of the memorandum of agreement between the college and the NHS trust on the placement of students and answer the following questions from the information in it:
>
> - If a student causes harm to a client being cared for in the Trust, who is liable for the student?
> - If the midwife tutor supervising the student gives negligent advice to the student and as a result the mother and baby suffer harm, who is liable for that harm? Is there a difference if the advice was given during the theoretical work in the college rather than in the clinical setting?
> - If the midwife tutor has her own case load and she fails to deal appropriately with a mother who has a delayed third stage and the mother suffers harm, who is liable?

Commentary
Liability for both tutor and student should be clarified in the memorandum of agreement. If it is not and you are unable to answer these questions from it, take up this with your manager or head of school and professional body/teacher's association.

One of the roles of the midwifery tutor is to act as a mentor for students providing advice and support over a wide area to ensure that the student is able to concentrate on her studies. This may mean that the tutor becomes involved in concern about failures to maintain clinical standards.

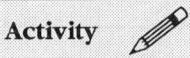

> **Activity**　　　　　　　　　　　　　　　　　　　　　　　　　　**30 minutes**
>
> A student reports to you that the standard of care being followed in the labour ward is not in accordance with the reasonable standard that would be expected.
>
> Identify the action which you would take and prepare guidelines for such a situation which could be used by other tutors.
>
> Use Appendix 3 to assist you in this activity.

Commentary
This is not an uncommon occurrence and the midwife tutor should be clear about her role in this. Clearly she should not indulge in useless gossip but if there are grave concerns about clinical practice reported by a student, she should ensure that these concerns are brought to the attention of the appropriate person.

Midwifery tutors/lecturers are usually employed by institutions of higher education, although some have dual appointments within universities and NHS Trusts. Alternatively some teachers have negotiated individual honorary contracts with an NHS trust.

For those lecturers who have not got formalized links with clinical areas, personal clinical practice would not be advisable. However supervision of students clinical practice is an integral part of the teachers role. This type of activity should be covered in the memorandum of agreement.

The lecturer has to comply with the laws which underpin midwifery practice. Therefore if substandard care is identified there is a duty to draw this to the attention of the supervisor of midwives and appropriate manager.

Communication with clinical areas are frequently difficult for lecturers based within institutes of higher education *but* without regular clinical activity the midwifery lecturer may find effective communication more difficult.

Approximately three per cent of all supervisors of midwives are employed as midwifery tutors/lecturers. The appointment of lecturers to this post offers one method of maintaining effective communication pathways between clinical practitioners and institutes of higher education.

Activity — *The timing will vary for this activity*

You are advising a student who is about to start a research project. The student is uncertain about getting started, getting approval, getting management support, clarifying publication rights, obtaining the consent of the client.

Draw up a protocol for the student which will ensure that all preliminary matters are considered at the beginning of the research.

Commentary
Table 30.8 gives a set of headings which you should find of assistance in this activity. Make sure that your protocol is user-friendly.

Preparing to be a preceptor

The introduction of the scheme of preceptorship should ensure that many practitioners are now involved in playing this role to assist their junior colleagues.

Activity — 30 minutes

Define the duties of a preceptor.

Commentary

As long ago as 1991 in the UKCC 'Report of the Post-registration Education and Practice Project' (PREPP), the role of the preceptor was discussed and promoted as,

> 'A preceptor should provide support for each newly qualified practitioner.' (p.19)

Informal support for newly registered midwives often exists but an ad hoc approach is not recommended. The UKCC suggest that preparation for this role is essential. The role of preceptor is associated with the provision of effective clinical supervision. Your local institute of higher education, school of nursing and midwifery or NHS trust personnel training department may provide appropriate education for this the role.

Useful further reading which explores the role of preceptor and the implications can be found in:

> Butterworth, T., Faugier, J. (1992). *Clinical Supervision and Mentorship in Nursing*. London: Chapman Hall.

Once you have reflected on the need for, and the qualities of a preceptor, this could become one of your personal professional objectives for the future.

Final endnote

At the end of this section you *have now completed* the unit covering the legal aspects of midwifery practice.

You should check with the objectives set out in the introduction to this unit to ensure that you have met them.

Ensure that you can provide documentary evidence of your reflections for inclusion within your Personal Professional Profile.

If you are seeking academic credits for elements within the workbook you will need to approach an appropriate institute of higher education for approved criteria for assessment.

This should not be seen however as the end of your involvement with the areas covered in this unit. In some ways this is only the end of the beginning or the end of the first stage. You must ensure that your understanding of the law relating to midwifery practice develops and remains up to date.

Future work

Other areas which have not been included in this study unit such as mental health law, legal aspects of complementary medicine, legal aspects of medicinal products, vaccinations and health promotion could also be studied in the future as part of the on-going professional development which all midwives have a personal duty to meet.

In addition new legislation is passed, decisions are made by judges which amend the common law or create new laws. Try and ensure that you keep up to date with the changes. Supplements will be issued from time to time as necessary to this workbook and the textbook. Midwives have a professional duty to maintain their competence and this would include understanding legal developments which affect the rights of the client/mother and child and also those which affect the professional accountability and practice of the midwife.

References

Butterworth, T., Faugier, J. (1992). *Clinical Supervision and Mentorship in Nursing*. London: Chapman Hall.

Dimond, B. (1994). 'In vitro fertilization and the law'. *Modern Midwife*, Vol. 4, No.12, pp.32–34.

Dimond, B. (1994). *Legal Aspects of Midwifery*. Hale: Books for Midwives Press.

Dimond, B. (1995). 'The scope of fertility treatment'. *Modern Midwife*, January, p.34.

UKCC (1991). *Report of the Post-Registration Education and Practice Project (PREPP)*. London: UKCC.

Bibliography

Dimond, B. (1994). *The Legal Aspects of Midwifery.* Hale: Books for Midwives Press.
Bolam v. *Friern Hospital Management Committee* (1957) 2 All ER 118.
Secretary of State v. *ASLEF* (No 2) [1972] 2 All ER 949.
Trade Union and Labour Relations (Consolidation) Act 1992 Section 238.
Trade Union and Labour Relations (Consolidation) Act 1992 Section 237.
Protecting Health Care Workers and Patients from Hepatitis B HSG(93)40 NHS Management Executive.
Dimond, B. (1994). 'Do practitioners owe greater loyalty to employers or patients'. *British Journal of Nursing,* Vol. 3, No. 22, pp.1155–56.
Department of Health (1993). *Expert Advisory Report of the Department of Health.* Chaired by Baroness Cumberlege. London: HMSO.
Walker v. *Northumberland County Council* Times Law Report 24 November 1994 Queens Bench Division.

Indicative reading

Department of Health (1994). *Being Heard. The Report of a Review Committee on NHS Complaints Procedures.* Chaired by Professor Alan Wilson, May, London: HMSO.
Health and Safety Commission (1993). *Management of Health and Safety at Work: Approved Code of Practice.* London: HMSO.
Mason, D., Edwards, P. (1993). *Litigation: A Risk Management Guide for Midwives.* London: RCM.

See also Recommended Reading List in the main textbook.

APPENDIX ONE

Personal Reflections and Planned Learning Activities Record

TYPE OF ACTIVITY
FROM SECTION ...... PAGE ...... OF THE WORKBOOK
TIME TAKEN ......

PERSONAL REFLECTIONS AND APPLICATION TO MY PERSONAL PRACTICE

CONTRIBUTION OF THIS ACTIVITY TO MY PROFESSIONAL DEVELOPMENT

ACTION PLAN

OUTCOME

Signed   Date

This form can be photocopied for inclusion in your personal professional profile.

APPENDIX TWO

Format for Reporting Cases of Alledged Misconduct by Practising Midwives to the LSA

Section 1

Name of midwife:
Pin number:
Date of registration as a midwife:
Home address:
Post held:
Place of employment:

Section 2

Allegations:

Section 3

Rules breached:

I. Code of Professional Conduct for the Nurses, Midwives and Health Visitors

II. Midwives Rules

III. A Midwife's Code of Practice

Section 4

Midwife's previous record:
Summary of incident/incidents occurred:
Action taken by Supervisor of Midwives:
Outcome of investigation:
Mitigating circumstances
Recommendation to Local Supervising Authority
Signed .... **Date** ....

APPENDIX THREE

Format for Systematic Evaluation of a Significant Incident or Professional Issue

---

1. Summary of incident/issue:

a) Personnel involved

b) Who is accountable for the activities surrounding this incident/issue?

c) Have any similar incidents occurred?

d) Other comments:

---

2. Possible allegations and/or professional implications:

a)

b)

c)

3. Mitigating circumstances:

4. Rules and Codes breached:
Identify the paragraph/s in the following UKCC Rules and Codes (UKCC 1996 Guidelines for professional practice will guide/assist your reflection).

a) Code of Professional Conduct for Nurses, Midwives and Health Visitors

b) Midwives Rules

c) A Midwife's Code of Practice

d) Scope of Professional Practice

e) Other UKCC advisory documents

Any other legal aspects to consider?

5. Possible actions to be requested by me or proposed to my Supervisor of Midwives

Please state:

    a)   Supportive action

    b)   Education activity

    c)   Disciplinary investigation

6. Outcome of this systematic evaluation of my practice:

Legal Aspects of Midwifery Workbook

7. Recommendations for my future professional practice

a)

b)

c)

d)

8. Outcome of this systematic evaluation for midwifery practice within the NHS Trust/Group practice

APPENDIX FOUR

Self Review Form for Practising Midwives

YOUR NAME..
SUPERVISOR OF MIDWIVES..

UKCC PIN   RENEWAL DATE

circle which applies

Are you required to practice in different care settings?   YES   NO

When completing this form please note that midwifery experience in all of these categories may not apply to you but a review of the experience available to you may become the focus of discussion.

THIS SECTION IS DESIGNED TO ASSIST YOU REVIEW YOUR PERSONAL MIDWIFERY PRACTICE

Please indicate if you are competent* to:

Please indicate any additional skills or knowledge needed in order to practice

*can demonstrate the necessary knowledge, skills and professional attitudes

Provide:	YES	NO	COMMENTS
Antenatal care	☐	☐	
Intrapartum care			
in normal labour	☐	☐	
in abnormal labour	☐	☐	
Postnatal care	☐	☐	
Neonatal care			
for normal neonates	☐	☐	
for transitional care infant	☐	☐	
for special care	☐	☐	
Integrated midwifery service	☐	☐	
Continuity of carer	☐	☐	
A service offering a named midwife for a defined client group	☐	☐	

Legal Aspects of Midwifery Workbook

PROFESSIONAL ISSUES AND SKILLS UPDATE REQUIREMENTS
This section provides you with the opportunity to identify aspects of practice which you *may* require updating.

Please indicate your needs:

	YES	NO
ADULT RESUSCITATION	☐	☐
NEONATAL RESUSCITATION	☐	☐
EPIDURAL TOP-UP PROCEDURE	☐	☐
INTRAVENOUS CANNULATION	☐	☐
PERINEAL SUTURING	☐	☐
UNPLANNED HOME BIRTH	☐	☐
DIFFERENTIAL DIAGNOSIS OF GYNAECOLOGICAL/ OBSTETRIC EMERGENCIES	☐	☐
PRENATAL SCREENING INFORMATION GIVING	☐	☐
PERINATAL DEATH SUPPORT/ COUNSELLING	☐	☐
FAMILY PLANNING INFORMATION UPDATE	☐	☐
CHILD PROTECTION ISSUES	☐	☐

PLEASE STATE OTHER NEEDS

Signed .... **Date** ....

Self Review Form for Practising Midwives

Following completion of the previous section you are invited to make an appointment with your named supervisor of midwives.

You are invited to have available the section in your Personal Professional Profile which provides evidence of your professional development, and the relevant UKCC documents.

Make a note of any specific professional and practice issues that you would like to discuss with your supervisor:

SUMMARY OF ISSUES TO BE TAKEN FORWARD:

Midwife's signature: Date:

Named supervisor's signature: Date:

Date of next meeting:

This form may be reproduced for inclusion in your personal professional profile

APPENDIX FIVE

Complaints about Professional Conduct

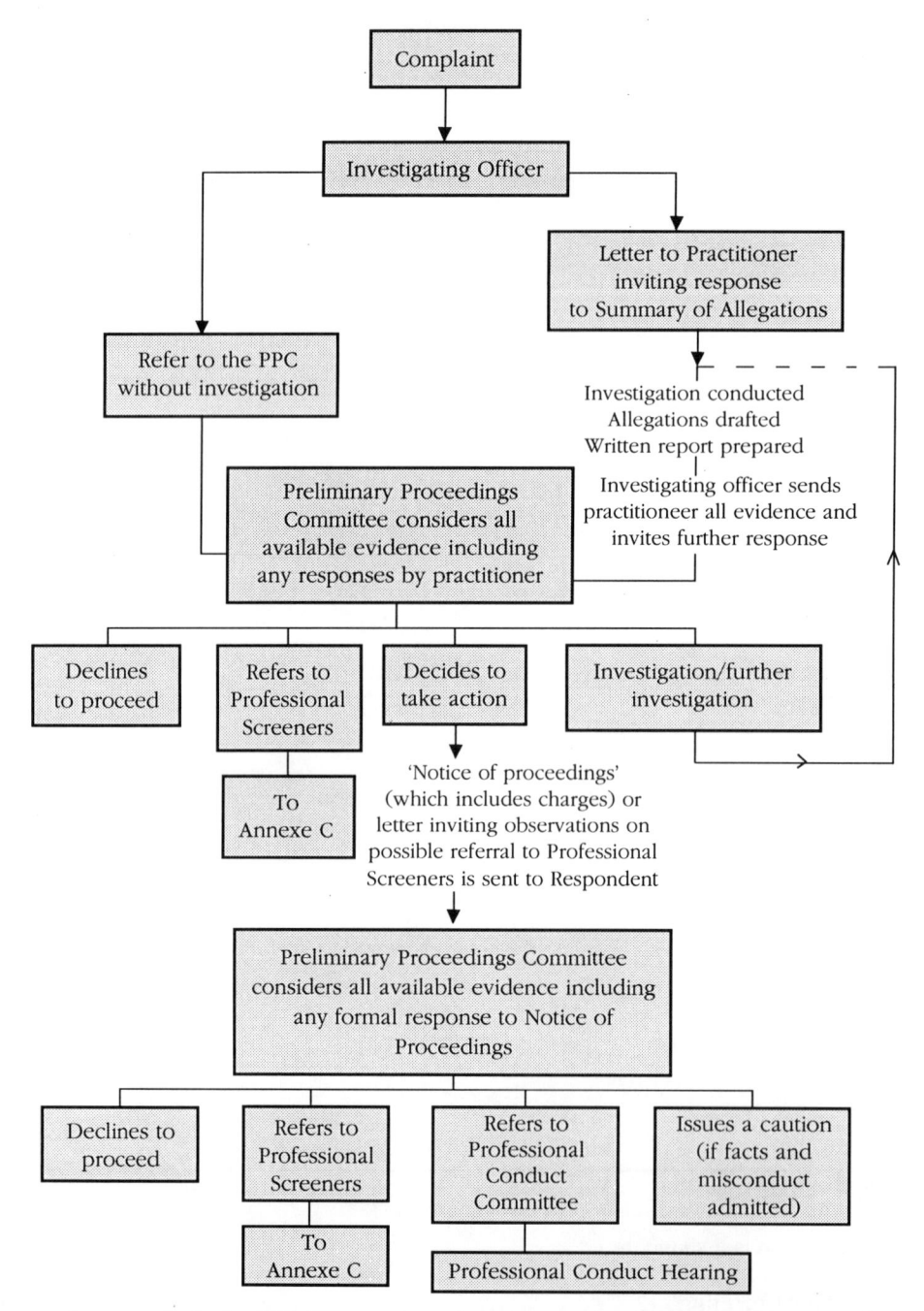

```
                        ┌──────────────┐
                        │  Complaint   │
                        └──────┬───────┘
                               ▼
                    ┌─────────────────────┐
          ┌─────────│ Investigating Officer│─────────┐
          │         └─────────────────────┘         │
          │                                         ▼
          │                           ┌──────────────────────────┐
          │                           │  Letter to Practitioner  │
          │                           │    inviting response     │
          │                           │  to Summary of Allegations│
          │                           └──────────────┬───────────┘
          ▼                                          ▼
┌──────────────────────┐              Investigation conducted
│ Refer to the PPC     │              Allegations drafted
│ without investigation│              Written report prepared
└──────────┬───────────┘              Investigating officer sends
           │                          practitioner all evidence and
           │                          invites further response
           ▼
┌───────────────────────────────┐
│  Preliminary Proceedings      │
│  Committee considers all      │
│  available evidence including │
│  any responses by practitioner│
└───────────────────────────────┘
```

Flow continues to four options:

- **Declines to proceed**
- **Refers to Professional Screeners** → To Annexe C
- **Decides to take action**
- **Investigation/further investigation**

'Notice of proceedings' (which includes charges) or letter inviting observations on possible referral to Professional Screeners is sent to Respondent

↓

Preliminary Proceedings Committee considers all available evidence including any formal response to Notice of Proceedings

Four options:

- **Declines to proceed**
- **Refers to Professional Screeners** → To Annexe C
- **Refers to Professional Conduct Committee** → Professional Conduct Hearing
- **Issues a caution** (if facts and misconduct admitted)

Annexe A: A simplified illustration of the process by which an allegation of misconduct is considered by the Preliminary Proceedings Committee

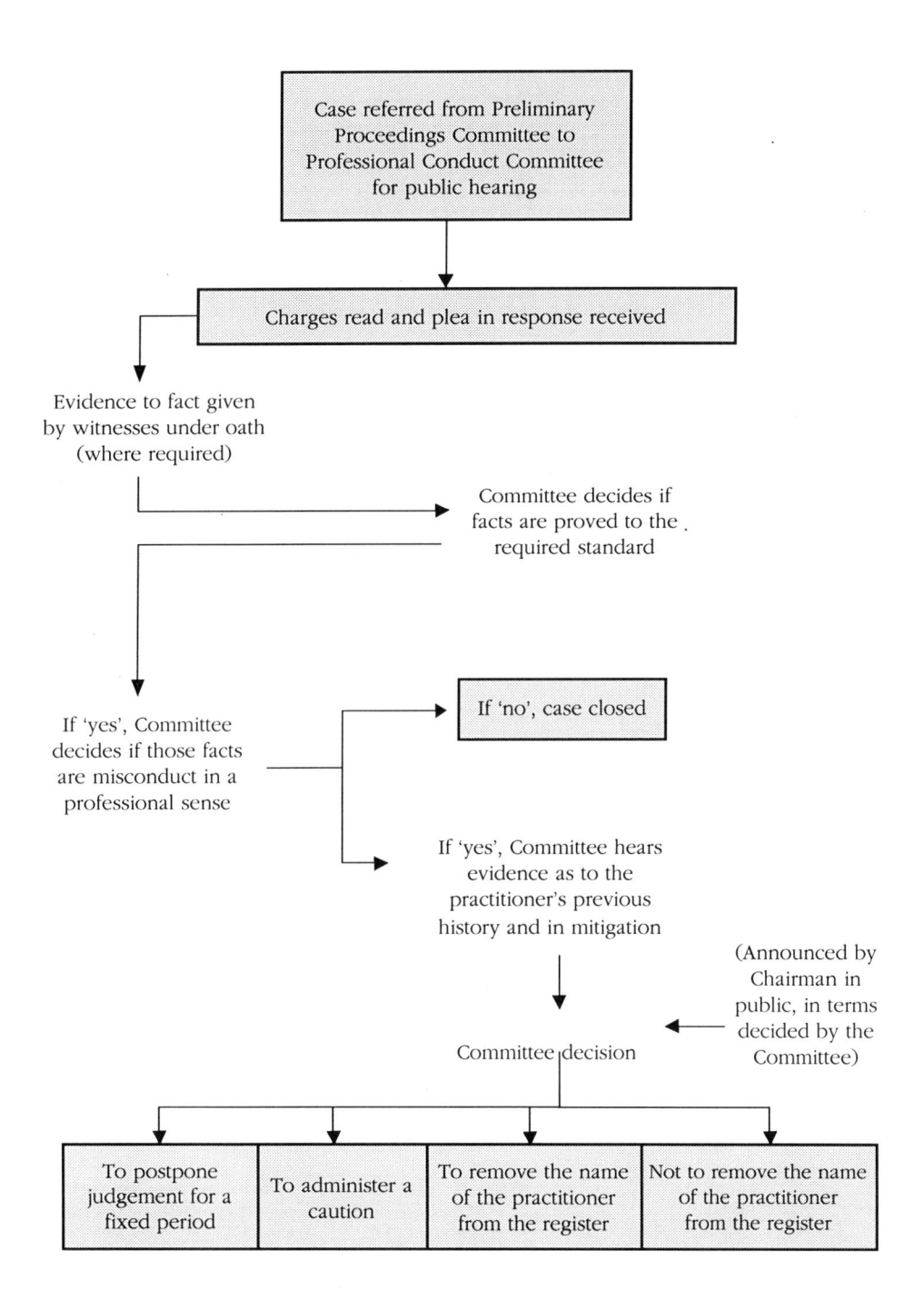

Complaints about Professional Conduct

```
┌─────────────────────────────┐
│  Case referred from Preliminary │
│  Proceedings Committee to   │
│  Professional Conduct Committee │
│       for public hearing    │
└─────────────────────────────┘
              │
              ▼
┌─────────────────────────────────────┐
│ Charges read and plea in response received │
└─────────────────────────────────────┘
              │
              ▼
Evidence to fact given
by witnesses under oath
    (where required)
              │
              ▼
        Committee decides if
        facts are proved to the
           required standard

If 'yes', Committee           ┌──────────────────┐
decides if those facts  ───▶  │ If 'no', case closed │
are misconduct in a           └──────────────────┘
professional sense

        If 'yes', Committee hears
        evidence as to the
        practitioner's previous
        history and in mitigation
                                        (Announced by
                                         Chairman in
                                         public, in terms
                                         decided by the
              Committee decision  ◀──────  Committee)
```

| To postpone judgement for a fixed period | To administer a caution | To remove the name of the practitioner from the register | Not to remove the name of the practitioner from the register |

Annexe B: A simplified illustration of the process by which an allegation of misconduct is considered by the Professional Conduct Committee

Legal Aspects of Midwifery Workbook

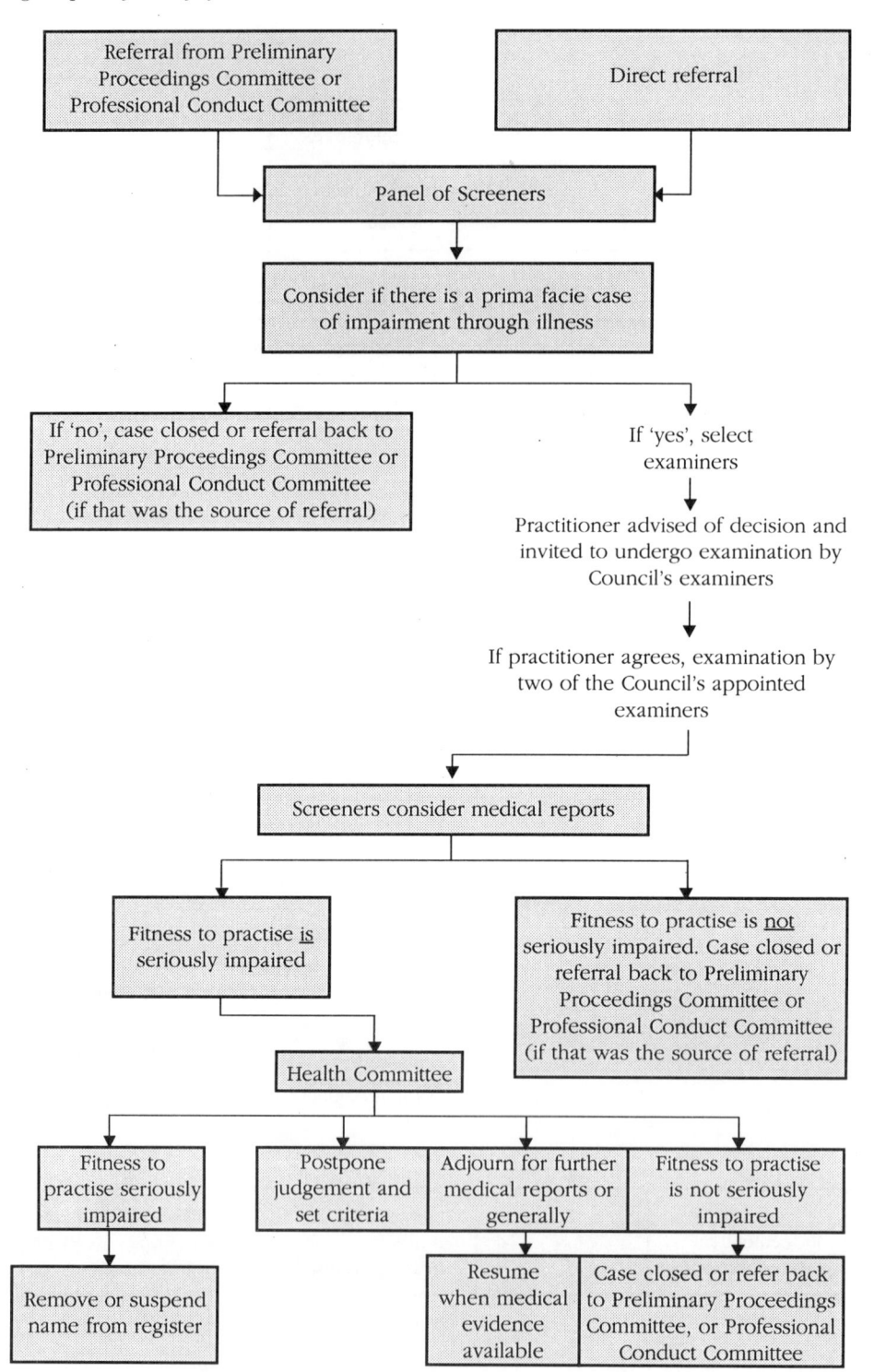

```
┌─────────────────────────┐         ┌─────────────────────────┐
│ Referral from Preliminary│         │                         │
│  Proceedings Committee or│         │     Direct referral     │
│ Professional Conduct     │         │                         │
│      Committee           │         │                         │
└───────────┬─────────────┘         └───────────┬─────────────┘
            │                                    │
            └────────►┌─────────────────────┐◄───┘
                     │  Panel of Screeners  │
                     └──────────┬──────────┘
                                ▼
                  ┌──────────────────────────────┐
                  │ Consider if there is a prima │
                  │ facie case of impairment     │
                  │ through illness              │
                  └──────┬───────────────┬───────┘
                         ▼               ▼
```

If 'no', case closed or referral back to Preliminary Proceedings Committee or Professional Conduct Committee (if that was the source of referral)

If 'yes', select examiners

↓

Practitioner advised of decision and invited to undergo examination by Council's examiners

↓

If practitioner agrees, examination by two of the Council's appointed examiners

↓

Screeners consider medical reports

| Fitness to practise *is* seriously impaired | Fitness to practise is *not* seriously impaired. Case closed or referral back to Preliminary Proceedings Committee or Professional Conduct Committee (if that was the source of referral) |

↓

Health Committee

Fitness to practise seriously impaired	Postpone judgement and set criteria	Adjourn for further medical reports or generally	Fitness to practise is not seriously impaired
Remove or suspend name from register		Resume when medical evidence available	Case closed or refer back to Preliminary Proceedings Committee, or Professional Conduct Committee

Annexe C: A simplified illustration of the process by which complaints alleging unfitness to practise are considered

Complementary Therapy and the Midwife

Bridgit Dimond identifies the legal issues arising for the midwife who undertakes training in complementary therapies and wishes to apply this in her practice

In her introduction to *Modern Midwife's* series on complementary therapies and midwifery practice, Denise Tiran emphasized the requirement that the midwife should keep up to date with contemporary practice by learning about complementary therapies and anticipating demand before it arises.[1] Here we identify the legal issues which arise and the implications for the professional accountability of the midwife, by looking at some examples of complementary therapies in midwifery.

The midwife can be involved in complementary medicine in two distinct ways.

- She may undertake the training in a specific therapy and wish to apply this to the practice of midwifery; *or*

- She may be caring for a client who wishes to use complementary therapies.

The midwife with qualifications in a complementary therapy

The UKCC recognizes that midwives may become qualified in non-traditional therapies. In the *Midwife's Code of Practice*,[2] paragraph 56 states that midwives may undertake qualifications in complementary or alternative therapies and may wish to apply this additional knowledge and skill in their practice. It emphasizes:

- The need for practice to be based on sound principles and all available and current knowledge and skill.

- The importance of consent by the mother to the use of such therapies.

- The personal accountability for her or his professional practice.

Similarly, the UKCC advice on *Standards for the Administration of Medicines*[3] states in paragraph 39 that 'Some registered nurses, midwives and health visitors, having first undertaken successfully a training in complementary or alternative therapy which involves the use of substances such as essential oils, apply their specialist knowledge and skill in their practice. It is essential that practice in these respects, as in others, is based upon sound principles, available knowledge and skill. The importance of consent to the use of such treatment must be recognized. So, too, must the practitioner's personal accountability for her or his professional practice'. Paragraph 38 gives advice on the administration of homeopathic or herbal substances. However, midwives wishing to observe these basic principles tread a minefield of legal problems.

Defining competence and standard of care

How is competence determined in a non-orthodox sphere of practice, and how is the standard of care defined? *The Scope of Professional Practice*[4] envisaged that registered practitioners could and should develop their practice safely if they followed the six principles set out in that guidance. However, one of the major difficulties for any practitioner advancing into a new field of practice is determining her/his own competence.

Under the principles of the extended role,[5] tasks were delegated by doctors to practitioners who had undertaken the appropriate training. This training was evidenced by certificates which were issued following assessment on a new activity. This meant that both the practitioner and her employer had some *prima facie* evidence of capacity. There is much to be said for this.

Many of the complementary therapies have an established professional body, with educational requirements and a clear system of assessment and competence. However, this does not, as yet, apply to them all. It is extremely difficult to establish competency in a field where there is no established professional body determining standards of practice. Water births are an example from midwifery practice.[6]

In the future, more of the non-traditional therapists will establish professional bodies with professional conduct proceedings and may eventually obtain registered status. For example, in 1993 the Osteopaths Act set up a registration body for osteopaths. Chiropractors have also obtained registration status.

Marks[7] has emphasized that potential purchasers of complementary medicines should proceed with extreme caution until each body has established statutory registration. In the meantime, competence develops with experience, reading research articles and practice. There are always difficulties in obtaining the relevant experience in a complementary therapy which cannot be practised before that experience is obtained.

As new therapies develop, there is not initially the expertise to determine the accepted standards of care and practice.

Standards for care

In traditional medicine, the standards which the courts have applied to decide if a practitioner is in breach of the duty of care is determined by what has come to be known as the Bolam Tests.[8] Judge McNair defined the standard of care expected as: 'the standard of the ordinary skilled man exercising and professing to have that special skill'. Problems arise in applying the Bolam tests to complementary therapies:

- Who determines the standards in a developing area?

- Is there a different standard for the registered midwife who becomes involved in complementary therapies?

- When practising a complementary therapy, would a midwife be expected to provide a higher standard of care than someone who has only trained as a complementary therapist?

- Could there be conflict between the two standards of practice?

Denise Tiran cites a situation where a father insists that his wife continues to receive acupuncture despite the onset of complications in labour.[1] In these circumstances, if the midwife, as a practitioner of acupuncture continued to provide that therapy when the 'reasonable midwife' would have taken different action, such as arranging for an obstetrician to attend, then the midwife would probably be in breach of her duty of care to the mother according to the Bolam Test.

Such conflicts between complementary therapies are likely to be rare but the midwife needs to be aware of the possibility and alert to the dangers. At the same time, she needs to keep up to date with revisions to the standards within relevant therapies.

Cummings[9] notes that there are positive research findings published on homeopathy, but none yet relates to midwifery. The midwifery profession could research the effectiveness of homeopathy in midwifery care. This comment could probably be applied to most of the alternative and complementary therapies, and midwives should encourage research-based practice.

Personal and vicarious liability

If a midwife is negligent in carrying out a complementary therapy and this causes harm to the mother or baby then she will be personally liable. If she practises as a self-employed midwife she will have to pay the compensation herself or through her insurance cover for professional indemnity.[10] If she is an employed midwife, her employer would be vicariously liable for her negligence.

However, vicarious liability depends upon whether she was acting in course of employment when she carried out the therapy. Say, for example, that a NHS Trust unwilling to fund training of midwives in alternative therapies issued instructions that a midwife should not carry out or be involved in these therapies in the course of midwifery practice, and the midwife refused to obey these instructions. Could the Trust then claim that in disobeying these orders the midwife was not acting in the course of employment and therefore the Trust was not vicariously liable?

Normally, disobeying orders does not remove an employee's actions from being in course of employment. An example from another branch of employment law is that of a tanker driver who lit a match (a forbidden act when loading or unloading a petrol tanker) and the subsequent fire destroyed the garage. Although the driver's activity (striking a match) was forbidden, it was still considered to have taken place in the course of his employment.[12] His employers were therefore vicariously viable for his actions and the cost of rebuilding the garage.

It would be possible to envisage a situation where the forbidden activity of the midwife meant that she was no longer acting in course of employment. For example, a Trust might forbid the use of aromatherapy in its hospitals. A midwife with training in this field might defy the Trust's instructions and bring her own oils into the hospital; she might offer a clinic outside the usual times and provide aromatherapy care for her clients. If harm resulted as a result of her negligent practice, the Trust might be able to establish that this was not performed as part of her course of employment and challenge any vicarious liability for the midwife's actions.

Conflict between the employer and UKCC guidelines

Would an employer's ban on the use of a complementary therapy be lawful or reasonable? What if the employer gives a registered practitioner instructions which appear to conflict with the guidance given by the UKCC?

This has happened in some recent cases, which have received media attention.

- Sister Pat Cooksley was dismissed by Plymouth Trust for copying a continuing drugs sheet which a doctor forgot to sign. Her dismissal was upheld by the internal disciplinary hearing, but proceedings for professional misconduct were not initiated by the UKCC. She was subsequently reinstated.

- Valerie Foster and Jill Kruzins, two midwives in East Herts Trust were disciplined after allowing a labour in water to progress to delivery in a home birth. This was against Trust policy. However, the mother herself wanted a water birth, and the UKCC advice emphasizes the importance of the client's wishes.

However, there has been no ruling by an Appeal Court over the circumstances in which it would be reasonable for a registered midwife to disobey instructions given by an employer as being in conflict with her duty set out in the professional advice from the UKCC. In practice, such conflicts should be rare, as purchasers require Trusts in the NHS agreements to ensure that registered staff observe the standards of professional practice.

Where the midwife acquires skills in a complementary therapy, it is essential that she discusses the use of these skills with her employer, senior managers and colleagues. There may be contra-indications to the use of some therapies in certain circumstances. Hypnotism may not work on all clients. Aromatherapy may not be appropriate for a client with allergies. Homeopathic medicines might be contraindicated in some people and acupuncture might not be acceptable to some clients. If the employer has accepted the value of their use in general, it would be more difficult to argue that the midwife using them was not acting in course of employment.

Existing conditions, such as hypertension, may require clients to stay on traditional medicines and risks might occur if they came off these in order to start on other substances prescribed as complementary medicines.

When a Trust not only accepts but encourages midwives to apply the skills they have acquired through a training in complementary medicine, it appears that clients can receive improved care.

Reed and Norfolk[13] describe the use of aromatherapy in the midwifery practice over two and a half years with the support of the Director of Midwifery Services and medical colleagues. In particular, they described the use of lavender in pain relief and as a relaxant in labour. A survey of the mothers found that the majority felt it was helpful and more than half found it had helped with pain relief. However, the authors comment that it was impossible to assess whether the use of aromatherapy shortened the duration of labour.

Consent of client

The midwife has a legal duty to obtain the consent of the mother to any procedures and to ensure that her wishes and choices are respected as far as possible.[14] This would equally apply where the registered midwife has a specific skill in complementary therapy.

Record keeping

As always, it is essential for the midwife to keep comprehensive clear records on any agreement with the mother over the use of complementary therapies and on the use which she actually makes of them. Her colleagues will thus have access to written information about any action taken by the midwife and the midwife will have full details recorded should she ever be challenged over the appropriate course of action.

KEY POINTS
- The UKCC recognizes that midwives may become qualified in non-traditional therapies.
- One of the major difficulties for a practitioner advancing into a new field of practice is determining her/his competence. As new therapies develop, there is not initially the expertise to determine the accepted standards of care and practice.
- Vicarious liability depends on whether the midwife is acting in the course of her employment when she is carrying out the therapy.
- The midwife has a legal duty to respect the mother's wishes and choices.
- It is essential for the midwife to keep comprehensive, clear records on any agreement with the mother over the use of complementary therapies.

References
1. Tiran, D. (1994). 'Complementary therapies and midwifery practice'. *Modern Midwife*, 4(9): pp.8-10.
2. UKCC (1994). *The Midwife's Code of Practice*. London: UKCC.
3. UKCC (1992). *Standards for the Administration of Medicines*. London: UKCC.
4. UKCC (1993). *The Scope of Professional Practice*. London: UKCC.
5. Dimond, B. (1994). 'Legal aspects of role expansion'. in Hunt, G., Wainwright, P. (Eds). *Expanding the Role of the Nurse*. Oxford: Blackwell Scientific Publications.
6. Dimond, B. (1994). 'Water births - the legal implications'. *Modern Midwife*, 4(1) pp.12-13.
7. Marks, V. (1992). *Health Direct*. 22: p.12.
8. Bolam v. Friern Hospital Management Committee (1957). *All Eng Law Rep*. 2(118) p.121.
9. Cummings, B. (1994). 'Using homeopathy in midwifery care'. *Modern Midwife*, 4(12) pp.17-20.
10. Dimond, B. (1994). 'Reliable or liable? Indemnity and insurance'. *Modern Midwife*, 4(4) pp.6-7.
11. Dimond, B. (1993). 'Vicarious liability'. *Modern Midwife*, 3(3) pp.10-11.
12. Century Insurance Company Ltd v. Northern Ireland Road Transport Board (1942). *All Eng Law Rep*. 1(509) p.1491.
13. Reed, L., Norfolk, L. (1993). 'Aromatherapy in midwifery'. *Int J Alt Comp Med*. 11(12) pp.15-17.
14. Re T [Adult: Refusal of Medical Treatment] (1992). *All Eng Law Report*. 4:649, Court of Appeal.

Reproduced with kind permission from Modern Midwife, February, 1995

Local Pay 1996/97: Guidance for Purchasers

1. Details of the recommendations in the 1996 reports of the NHS Pay Review Bodies and Government decisions on implementation were sent to you by Aileen Simkins on 8 February. We are waiting to give guidance to purchasers on their role in introducing local pay successfully in the NHS.

3. 1995 was a difficult year with protracted pay negotiations at national and local level but the result was that around 93 per cent of NHS staff had part of their pay determined locally, resulting in fair and affordable increases. It is important to build on this in 1996, with local pay forming part of trusts' strategies for delivering high quality patient services through a well motivated workforce. Purchasers should support trusts as employers in developing their management approach to pay, and other human resource policies, and should not carry out their financial and contracting responsibilities in a way which implies that local pay means low awards which might be held to be unfair by both staff and the public.

Resources in 1996/97

4. Local pay increases in 1996/97 must be affordable. The context is that the Public Expenditure Settlement for HCHS revenue for 1996/97 gave 1.1 per cent real terms increase and a 3.9 per cent cash increase. In addition, health services are expected to increase their efficiency by at least 3 per cent, including savings to be realized by reductions in the management costs of trusts and authorities. The overall resourcing position will allow for further improvements in services and reasonable pay awards.

Action needed

5. 1996/97 is a key year in the process of consolidating the transition to locally negotiated pay increases for staff on national terms and conditions. Purchasers will be discussing with providers the implications of the Pay Review Body reports for their contracted activities and prices, and are asked:

- to conduct any public discussion of pay funding in a way which protects the employers' negotiating position

- to build on the collaborative approach with providers which is essential if the long term benefits of the shift to local pay are to be achieved

- to recognize that providers prices may need to incorporate the costs of structural changes which will be helpful to all parties in the longer term

- in negotiating quality standards and activity targets, to ensure that trusts can secure these through effective human resources policies including fair pay increases, taking into account the need to recruit and retain staff.

Enquiries
7. Any enquiries about this guidance should be addressed to Mrs Pat Urry in Room 2E40, Quarry House (Tel: 0113 2545773).

EL(96)9

Midwifery-managed Units

One of the major innovations in maternity care expected to follow *Changing Childbirth* is the establishment of midwifery-managed units, but **Bridgit Dimond** finds there are many 'what if...?' questions to be answered before midwives take up this challenge

The establishment of midwifery-managed units away from district general hospitals has great significance for the role and training of the midwife, and midwives naturally have many concerns about such units being established.

Midwives who have been consulted on setting up such a unit were given the opportunity to air their fears. The unit would not have theatres or 24-hour obstetric cover and would be comparable to a home birth. The midwives were asked to write down anonymously their worries and the legal implications of these were considered.

Risks

Risk management and assessment were considered in *Modern Midwife*[1] as part of the health and safety regulations. However, the same techniques can be used in planning the operational policy of a midwife-managed unit, in determining the client group and in deciding upon the equipment, supplies (e.g. drugs, blood) and the staffing levels necessary to operate safely. Table 1 sets out the type of risks which worried the midwives.

The risks cited are probably no different from those which would be cited by midwives working in a district general hospital. However, the fear in a midwife-managed unit is whether there would be the resources necessary to cope and whether transfers could be effected in time.

Table 1. Risks which concern midwives

Risks to mothers
What if...?

- A woman has a huge haemorrhage and it is not possible to site an intravenous line to administer fluid and she dies? Or in the same situation, the bleeding continues after the IV is set up? And in the same situation, the mother is too ill to be transferred by ambulance?

- Something goes wrong when administering a pudendal block?

- There is retained placenta bleeding?

- The mother suddenly collapses and is too ill to be moved?

- The woman has a life-threatening problem such as postpartum haemorrhage or is fitting and is too unstable to be transferred?

Risks to baby
What if...?

- There is a cord prolapse and the baby is stillborn?

- An unbooked client arrives on our doorstep, fully dilated with the baby only 28 weeks?

- The fetal heart is heard in second stage but is delivered of a fresh stillbirth?

- The baby is flat at delivery and resuscitation and intubation are attempted but are unsuccessful?

- There is an unexpected stillbirth?

Many of the risks are foreseeable, but the reduction of risk does rely upon a high standard of antenatal screening to identify who should be delivered in a district general hospital unit. Even with the most efficient screening, emergencies would still arise. Chief concerns are the possibility of unexpected haemorrhaging or prolapse of the cord. Provisions can be made to deal with these emergencies, which would include higher levels of training for midwives in the resuscitation of the newborn, in the siting of cannulae and giving intra-venous substances and in the administration of a wider range of medicines than those currently agreed. As a result of the study, several working parties were established to draw up procedures, policies and preparations to meet these risks.

From this point of view of legal liability, if there is no evidence at antenatal stage which suggests that a woman should be delivered in a district general hospital and something goes wrong, provided all reasonable care has been taken and all reasonable action carried out to meet foreseeable risks, and those actions performed by the midwife in accordance with the Bolam Test,[2] then there is unlikely to be a successful civil action. However, much depends upon the evidence which is given and for this the records of the midwife are extremely important.

Transfers

The concerns expressed by midwives about transfers to hospital are set out in Table 2. Adequate planning of transfer could allay their fears about the associated risks.

On the transport side this would include the provision of ambulance transport with a paramedical team trained in obstetric emergencies, and specially equipped to cover all foreseeable emergencies. Training for midwives would have to cover the signs to watch for indicating the need for a transfer.

Table 2. Fears relating to transfer

What if...?

- The mother delivers an abnormal baby who dies in transit (the baby's abnormality might prevent resuscitation)?

- There is a cord prolapse and the baby dies during the transfer?

- The mother needs to be transferred because of the postpartum haemorrhage but the district general hospital has no empty beds and is unable to take the transfer, or harm occurs to the mother and baby while an empty bed is being sought?

- The registrar refuses to admit the mother following transfer?

- The mother refuses to be transferred?

- The baby is stillborn following fetal distress during transfer?

- Something goes wrong after transfer? Will the medical staff blame the midwives for not acting quickly enough? Or if a doctor disagreed in retrospect with the midwife's decisions or some aspect of her care, after transfer to the doctor, what would the midwife's position be legally?

- A problem occurs during transfer by ambulance, such as eclampsia or haemorrhage?

- There is a GP booking and a problem occurs during labour and the GP asks to transfer the care of the patient to a consultant - what is the midwife's position?

- The baby is born in the ambulance and dies because of lack of facilities?

- There is no adequate 24-hour transport for emergency transfers?

- A midwife is criticized by a consultant after the transfer of a baby with fetal distress and told 'I told you so'?

Is the midwife responsible for what happens in transit even after the medical staff are notified that it is taking place?

Establishing good communications with theatre staff in the district general hospital would be vital so that, as soon as an obstetric emergency arose, the appropriate action could be taken within the hospital to avoid delay. This would mean acceptance by hospital and theatre staff of instructions from the midwifery unit that an obstetric emergency was being transferred. Midwives were concerned that delays could result from red tape, such as the need for a particular reason to authorise the transfer. They reckoned that even when a confinement was taking place within the hospital, there might be a delay of as long as 30 minutes to prepare for a caesarean section.

Liaison with obstetricians

Midwives managing a midwife unit must have the cooperation and support of their obstetric colleagues and any element of competition or conflict must be removed. Some midwives feared that they would be criticized for their handling of the delivery by obstetricians in front of clients and that they would have little protection against such contempt. Every effort must be made to ensure joint planning between the professions, including pharmacists and physiotherapists, to ensure the highest standard of care for the client. Policies relating to the suitability of clients for the unit, and to the transfer of those at risk, are essential before the unit can begin its operation.

Refusals by clients

The philosophy behind the Winterton[3] and Cumberlege[4] Reports is that the mother should have more choice and her wishes should be taken into account. However, midwives fear that mothers might insist upon inappropriate treatment, care or place of confinement which could endanger the life of both mother and child. An earlier article in *Modern Midwife*[5] set out the legal principles relating to the right of the mother to give or refuse consent. One of the aims of a midwife-led service is that the relationship between mother and midwife will be much improved so that a mother develops respect for the judgement of the midwife and there is less likely to be conflict between the two. A birth plan can be agreed, with the mother recognizing when departure from the agreed plan is necessary.

Can the mother insist on delivery in a midwife-managed unit even though she is assessed as being a high-risk case? The answer is no. The managers of the unit have the right to determine who will be admitted and can refuse admission to a mother who is high-risk. They can also enforce a policy that only those who have been booked into the unit by the midwives are entitled to be delivered there. This would prevent ambulances bringing inappropriate patients to the unit. Table 3 sets out some of the ways in which a client might refuse to follow the advice of the midwife.

Table 3. Clients' refusals

What if...?

- A transfer is required, and the mother refuses to agree?
- A high-risk mother comes to the unit who has not been booked in there, but who refuses to be transferred to the hospital?
- The mother refuses to be transferred, is delivered in the unit and the baby is stillborn?
- During antenatal care, the mother needs to be transferred to consultant care and she refuses?
- The mother refuses fetal monitoring?
- She refuses to be transferred when there are problems in labour?
- A high-risk mother who is unsuitable for delivery in a midwifery-led unit insists on being delivered in the unit?
- A mother who requires obstetric intervention refuses to be moved and she and her partner want the flying squad to attend in the unit?
- The mother refuses syntometrine?

As the hospital is seen as the safety net when obstetric problems occur, it is not surprising that one of the major fears of the midwives was the possibility that mothers could refuse to be transferred and would not accept the midwife's judgement that such a transfer was essential. Allied to this was the worry that some mothers would use the unit inappropriately, attempting to be delivered there even when their antenatal care had shown that they were in a high-risk category and needed to be in hospital.

Indemnity and litigation

There is a feeling that if the midwife follows the professional guidelines and does all she reasonably can to ensure that the mother and baby are safe, then she is entitled to receive the loyalty and protection of the management. At present we have a system of fault liability and, unless the person bringing the action can show that there was fault (that is, the defendant was in breach of the duty of care), litigation will not be successful. However, this does not mean that the death or injury of a baby will not lead to litigation. Table 4 sets out these concerns.

In practical legal terms this means that, if litigation is brought, the midwife should be protected and indemnified by the management. This is actually what happens. Employed midwives are covered by vicarious liability of the employer for any negligence of the midwife while acting in the course of employment. This means that even if the writ is issued personally against the midwife, the employer should assist the midwife in the defence and agree that, if any compensation is payable, the employer will pay. Since 1948 the health authorities have accepted responsibility for the negligence of its non-medical and non-dental staff. Since January 1990 the health authority or NHS Trust has accepted

Table 4. Concerns about indemnity and litigation

- Do I have to take out medical insurance cover?

- What if parents take legal action after I have done everything which I should have done?

- Can new legal contracts be drawn up to give more cover to midwives in a midwife-managed unit?

- What form of legal back-up would be provided by the health authority/NHS Trust? Would this be provided in writing to each midwife?

- What guarantees and protection would be given by the health authority/NHS Trust in court?

- As this is a pioneering venture, would there be specific, written cover for midwives in the event of a catastrophe, as long as they had acted according to the rules?

- If a baby is delivered with an abnormality that could have been detected during the antenatal period, can the family blame the midwife involved?

liability for doctors and dentists. This means that there is no need for the employed midwife to take out insurance cover for negligence which occurs while she is acting in the course of employment.

Midwives, however, would like to have this legal situation set out in writing in their contract of employment. In practice, this is not necessary since it would be implied in the contract by law.

Even when there is no apparent negligence on the part of the midwife but she is facing a complaint or litigation, then she is entitled to receive the support of her employer. This would mean that the NHS Trust's solicitors should advise her on defending the claim and on making a statement and give her a briefing before any court hearing.

Prescribing, training and updating

There was concern that the necessary additional training would not be given to ensure that midwives were competent for this enhanced role. There was also a fear that, even if initial training were provided, there would not be an ongoing commitment to ensure regular revision. In this respect, midwives are more fortunate than other practitioners because there is a statutory requirement for them to be kept updated. This means that midwives could have a guarantee that revision will be provided, and there is no reason why an NHS Trust could not build this into their contract of employment.

Conclusions

Any attempt to go along the path of midwife-managed units involves risks. Extensive detailed planning can eliminate most of those risks but, at the end of the day, there may still be stillbirths and maternal deaths, though these occur even when the confinement takes place in hospital. Ultimately the decision must be given to the mother - if it is reasonable for her to be delivered at home or in a managed unit, then she should have the choice. Childbirth should be seen as a non-medical event except in those exceptional cases which require obstetric intervention. The UKCC[6] provides the principles for the professional development of the midwife to take responsibility in these units.

KEY POINTS

Midwives involved in the establishment of a midwifery-managed unit were given the opportunity to express their concerns anonymously. The principle areas of concerns they identified were:

- Risks to mother and baby
- Transfers from the unit to the district general hospital
- Refusals by clients
- Indemnity, litigation and protection by management
- Prescribing, training and updating.

References

1. Dimond, B. (1994). 'The midwife and risk management at work'. *Modern Midwife*, 4(4) pp.36–37.
2. House of Commons Select Committee (1992). *Second Report on the Maternity Services*. Vol. 1 (Winterton report). London: HMSO.
3. Bolam v. Friern Barnet Hospital Management Committee (1957). *All Engl Law Rep.* 2, p.118
4. Expert Maternity Group (1993). *Changing Childbirth* (Cumberlege Report). London: HMSO.
5. Dimond, B. (1993). 'Client autonomy and choice'. *Modern Midwife,* 3(1) pp.15–16.
6. UKCC (1992). *The Scope of Professional Practice.* London: UKCC.

Reproduced with kind permission from Modern Midwife, June, 1994

Medication and the Midwife: Statutory Control

In the first of two articles on the legal aspects of medication **Bridgit Dimond** examines the statutory framework which has been set up for the control of medicinal products

Compared with nurses and health visitors, midwives have extended powers for prescribing and administrating medicines.

The two main Acts of Parliament controlling the administration and use of medicines are The Medicines Act 1968 (Figure 1) and the Misuse of Drugs Act 1971.

These are supplemented by the *Midwives Rules* [1] (which were slightly amended in November 1993) which also have statutory force. In addition the *Midwife's Code of Practice* [2] (recently revised) gives advice on the implementation of Rule 41 (Figure 2).

Figure 1. Classification of medicines under the Medicines Act 1968

Pharmacy-only products
These can only be sold or supplied retail by someone conducting a retail pharmacy when the product must be sold for a registered pharmacy by, or under the supervision of, a registered pharmacist.

General sales list
These are medicinal products which may be sold other than from a retail pharmacy so long as the provisions relating to section 53 of the Medicines Act are complied with. This means that the place of sale must be the premises where the business is carried out; they must be capable of excluding the public; the medicines must have been made up elsewhere and the contents must not have been opened since make-up.

Prescription-only list
These medicinal products are only available on a practitioner's prescription. Schedule I of the Regulation's lists the prescription-only products and Part II of the schedule lists the prescription-only products which are covered by the Misuse of Drugs Act 1971.

Figure 2. Rule 41: Administration of medicines and other forms of pain relief [1]

1. A practising midwife shall not on her own responsibility administer any medicine, including analgesics, unless in the course of her training, whether before or after registration as a midwife, she has been thoroughly instructed in its use and is familiar with its dosage and methods of administration or application.

2. A practising midwife shall not on her own responsibility administer any inhalational analgesic by the use of any type of apparatus unless:

- That apparatus is the time being approved by the Council on the recommendation of the Board as suitable for use by a midwife.

- That the midwife has ensured that the apparatus has been properly maintained.

3. Unless special exemption is given by the Council on the recommendations of a Board to enable a particular hospital to investigate new methods,

> a practising midwife must not administer any form of pain relief by the use of any type of apparatus or by any other means which has not been approved by the Council otherwise than on the instructions of a registered medical practitioner (*until such methods have been approved by the Council for midwives to undertake on their own responsibility and in accordance with paragraph (1) of this rule deleted under amendments 1993*)

The Code is not itself binding in law, but any failure to follow it would be taken into account in the hearing of an allegation of professional misconduct. Like all other practitioners registered by the United Kingdom Central Council for Nursing, Health Visiting and Midwifery (UKCC), the midwife is subject to the Council's guidance.[3-6]

The Medicines Act 1968

This Act set up an administrative and licensing system to control the sale and supply of medicines to the public, retail pharmacies and the packing and labelling of medicinal products.

Misuse of Drugs Act 1971

This Act and subsequent legislation makes provision for the classification of controlled drugs and their possession, supply and manufacture.

The Act makes it a criminal offence to carry on the manufacture, supply and possession of controlled drugs contrary to the regulations. Controlled drugs are divided into three categories:

- Class A includes: cocaine, diamorphine, morphine, opium, pethidine and class B substances when prepared for injection.
- Class B includes: oral amphetamines, barbiturates, cannabis, codeine.
- Class C includes: most benzodiazepines, meprobamate.

The Misuse of Drugs Regulations 1985 divides controlled drugs into five schedules, each specifying the requirements governing activities such as import, export, production, supply, possession, prescribing and record-keeping. These regulations enable the registered midwife, for the practice of her profession or employment, to possess and administer any controlled drug which the Medicines Act 1968 permits her to administer. Supplies may be made to her or possessed by her on the authority of a midwife's supply order duly signed by an appropriate medical officer. The Regulations also require her to maintain a register in which she must enter her details of each transaction of obtaining or administering the drug.

Midwives Rules

Rule 41 details further legally binding regulations in relation to the administration of medicines by midwives (Figure 2).

Rule 42 of the *Midwives Rules* requires the midwife to keep records in relation to medicines (Figure 3).

> **Figure 3. Rule 42: Records**
>
> 1. A practising midwife shall keep as contemporaneously as is reasonable detailed records of observations, care given and medicine or other forms of pain relief administered by her to all mothers and babies.
>
> 2. The records referred to in paragraph (1) of this rule shall be kept:
>
> - In the case of a midwife employed by a health authority or NHS trust in accordance with any directions given by her employer.
> - In any other case, in a form approved by the local supervising authority.

Reference must also be made to the UKCC *Standards for the Administration of Medicines* and *Standards for Records and Record Keeping*.[4,5]

The Midwife's Code of Practice

Paragraphs 24-38 of the new *Code of Practice* expand upon the midwife's duty in relation to medicines and analgesics.

This is the framework within which the midwife carries out her responsibilities in relation to medicines and medicinal products, and record-keeping.

Figure 4: Midwife's Code of Practice (recent revisions shown in italics)[2]

Medicines including analgesics

Supply, possession and use of controlled drugs

24. The possession and administration of controlled drugs by midwives is covered by the Misuse of Drugs Regulations 1985 (SI 1985 No 2066); the Misuse of Drugs (Northern Ireland) Regulations 1986 (SI 1986 No 52); and the Medicines Act 1968.

25. The Misuse of Drugs Regulations provide for the supply of pethidine to midwives (and any other controlled drug listed in Schedule 3 Parts 1 and 111 of the Medicines (Products other than Veterinary Drugs) (Prescription Only) Order 1983, SI 1983 No 1212 and subsequent orders using the supply order procedure. *Supply order forms can be obtained from your supervisor of midwives.*

26. The administration of controlled drugs by a midwife working in a hospital/institution should be in accordance with locally agreed policies and procedures. It may be decided locally that midwives practising in hospitals/institutions may follow the same practice as midwives working in the community.

Destruction of controlled drugs obtained by a midwife through a supply order procedure

27. Regulation 26 of Misuse of Drugs Regulations contains a procedure for witnessing the destruction of pethidine (or other controlled drugs approved in accordance with the Medicines Act 1968) which have been supplied to the midwife but which are no longer required. The destruction is done by the midwife but only in the presence of an 'authorized person'.

Surrender of controlled drugs

28. There is provision within the Misuse of Drugs Regulations for midwives to surrender stocks of unwanted controlled drugs to the pharmacist from whom they were obtained or to an appropriate medical officer, but not to a supervisor of midwives.

Controlled drugs obtained by a woman on prescription from a family practitioner for use in home confinement

29. In the case of controlled drugs supplied direct to the mother on a prescription from a family practitioner, the responsibility for destruction of any which are unused is that of the mother to whom in law they belong. In such a situation a midwife should advise the mother to destroy the drugs and may suggest that she does so in the presence of the midwife. The advice given by the midwife and any action taken should be recorded in the mother's notes, together with the details of the nature and the amounts of drugs involved.

References

1. UKCC (1993). *Midwives Rules*. London: UKCC.
2. UKCC (1994). *The Midwife's Code of Practice*. London: UKCC.
3. UKCC (1992). *Code of Professional Conduct*. London: UKCC.
4. UKCC (1992). *Standard for the Administration of Medicines*. London: UKCC.
5. UKCC (1993). *Standards for Records and Record Keeping*. London: UKCC.
6. UKCC (1989). *Exercising Accountability*. London: UKCC.

Reproduced with kind permission from Modern Midwife, October, 1994

The Midwife's Power to Prescribe

Bridgit Dimond continues her review of midwives and medication by considering the midwife's powers to prescribe

The Medicinal Products (Prescription by Nurses etc.) Act 1992 came into force in October 1994 with the introduction of pilot nurse-prescribing schemes.

However, it is unlikely that the provisions will affect the work of midwives since one of the comments of the Crown report which advocated nurse-prescribing was:

'We are aware that special arrangements for prescribing currently apply to midwives and occupational health nurses working in the community. We would not wish to disrupt their practice which is well-established and already clearly defined. It is not our intention that their position should be affected by the recommendations which follow'.[1]

For a long time, midwives have enjoyed considerable powers to determine the appropriate medicines to be given to a client and the right to prescribe them. Last month, I discussed the statutory framework in relation to control and destruction of drugs.[2] The paragraphs from *The Midwives Code of Practice* covering the supply of prescription-only medicines are shown in Figure 1.[3]

All practising midwives should have an up-to-date copy of the *British National Formulary (BNF)*.[4] At the front of the book there is a very useful introductory section which gives guidance on prescribing for different categories of drugs and different groups of patients. The *Nurse Prescribers' Formulary* has been published as supplement to the BNF.

Figure 1. Prescription-only and other medicines used by midwives[2]

Recent revisions (May 1994) are shown in italics

30. Certain medicines which are normally only available on prescription issued by a medical practitioner may be supplied to midwives who have notified their intention to practise for use in their practice under the Medicines Act 1968, either from a retail chemist or hospital pharmacy.

31. These medicines are listed in Schedule 3 Parts I and III of the Medicines (Products Other than Veterinary Drugs) (Prescription Only) Order 1983, SI No 1212 and any subsequent orders.

32. A midwife in the course of her practice in the community may need to carry antiseptics, sedatives and analgesics, local anaesthetics, oxytocic preparations and approves agents for neonatal and maternal resuscitation. The particular *medicines and* controlled drugs and medicines which a midwife may use will be determined locally *in collaboration with the senior midwife and medical and pharmaceutical staff and should be listed in written local policy*. A midwife should obtain details from her supervisor of midwives.

33. Return of prescription-only medicines to the supplying pharmacist should be receipted and recorded in the midwife's records. Disposal of prescription-only and other medicines should be recorded in the midwife's records.

34. *Homeopathic and herbal medicines are subject to the licensing provisions of the Medicines Act 1968, although those on the market when that Act became operative (which applies to most of the substances now available) received product licences without*

any evaluation of their efficacy, safety and quality. You should ensure that you are familiar with the requirements of Rule 41(1) in relation to the administration of medicines. It is necessary, however, to respect the right of individuals to self-administer substances of their choice.

35. *When a mother wishes to receive medicines of this kind and you believe that the substances might either be an inappropriate response to the presenting symptoms or likely to negate or enhance the effect of prescribed medicines, you have a duty to discuss this fully with the mother. The midwife, acting in the interests of the mother and in her full knowledge, should consider contacting the relevant expert practitioner to seek advice, but must also be mindful of the need not to overrule the woman's rights. (See also paragraph 55 on complementary and alternative therapies, which are NOT subject to the provisions of the Medicines Act 1968.)*

Administration of controlled drugs and medicines

36. *When administering* controlled drugs and other medicines in the NHS you should comply with locally agreed health authority *(or NHS Trust)* policies and procedures. In some authorities such policies may include a standing order signed by a consultant *registered medical* practitioner and a senior midwife authorizing the administration of controlled drugs and medicines for the use by the midwife in her practice in an institution. Those drugs and medicines would be similar to those carried by a midwife in her practice in the community.

37. *If you are* practising outside the area of *your* employing authority or *outside* the NHS, *you* should seek advice from *your* supervisor of midwives regarding any matters related to the supply, administration, storage, surrender and destruction of controlled drugs and other medicines.

38. Supervisors of midwives should periodically audit the records of controlled drugs and prescription only medicines kept by midwives. Any discrepancies must be investigated.

Prescribing in pregnancy

The *BNF* points out that 'drugs can have harmful effects on the fetus at any time during pregnancy. Experience with many drugs in pregnancy is limited'. In Appendix 4 it lists the drugs which are to be avoided or used with caution in pregnancy. It also makes the following recommendation.

'Drugs should be prescribed only if the expected benefit to the mother is thought to be greater than the risk to the fetus, and all the drugs should be avoided if possible during the first trimester. Drugs which have been extensively used in pregnancy and appear to be usually safe should be prescribed in preference to new or untried drugs; and the smallest effective doses should be used... Absence from the drug list does not imply safety'.[4]

Occasionally a heroic story is told of a sacrifice of a mother for her unborn baby. One such is that of Michelle Doyle who gave birth to a healthy boy after being told soon after she became pregnant that she was suffering from ovarian cancer. She refused cytotoxic drugs knowing that they would have harmed the baby. After the birth of the baby she had surgery for the cancer but it was too late to save her life.[5]

Such sacrifices cannot be insisted upon and, as the law stands at present, the mother can take medications which are necessary to save her life, even if they are likely to be harmful to the child. She is breaking criminal law only if she takes the drugs intending to cause a miscarriage.

Reference must also be made to the UKCC's Standards for the Administration of Medicines.[6]

Specific problems

Safety of the midwife carrying drugs
The midwife faces considerable danger if it is known that she carries controlled drugs in her bag. The preferred practice is for the mother to obtain any such drugs where necessary on prescription and retain them in her own home.

Drug addicts
What action does a midwife take if she discovers one of the women in her care is a drug addict?

If a doctor has reasonable grounds to believe a person is addicted to controlled drugs, then under the Misuse of Drugs (Notification of and Supply to Addicts) Regulations 1973, he is required to notify the Chief Medical Officer at the Home Office within seven days.

If a midwife suspects that one of her clients is addicted, she should ensure that a medical practitioner is informed and that the requisite details are sent to the Home Office. At present there are no laws in the UK which can permit action to be taken against the mother to prevent the fetus being harmed by the drugs (although there have been cases in the USA where pregnant drug addicts have been compelled to choose between a prison sentence and a detoxification programme). Nor can the fetus be made a ward of court before it is born.

Negligence and drugs
If a midwife makes an error in the prescription or administration of drugs she could face both criminal and civil proceedings. She would also face a professional conduct hearing by the Professional Conduct Committee of the UKCC and also disciplinary proceedings by the employer if she is employed.

Community and hospital supply
At present, although the midwife working in hospital has some powers in relation to the supply of drugs as her community counterpart, little advantage is taken of this, and the midwife is more likely to work with the obstetric medical staff who write up the client's drug sheet. The development of midwife-managed units may lead to more extensive use by midwives of their powers to supply drugs.

References
1. Department of Health (1989). *Report of the Advisory Group on Nurse Prescribing.* London: HMSO.
2. Dimond, B. (1994). 'The midwife and medication: statutory control'. *Modern Midwife*, Vol.4, No.10, pp.34-35.
3. UKCC (1994). *The Midwife's Code of Practice.* UKCC: London:
4. British Medical Association/Royal Pharmaceutical Society (1994). *British National Formulary.* London: British Medical Association/Royal Pharmaceutical Society.
5. (1994). *The Times.* 19 March.
6. UKCC (1992). *Standards for the Administration of Medicines.* London: UKCC.

Reproduced with kind permission from Modern Midwife, November, 1994

In vitro Fertilization and the Law

Bridgit Dimond considers the laws covering the use of embryos and gametes in human research and treatment for fertility

In 1992, there were 2,318 live births[1] in the United Kingdom as a result of *in vitro* fertilization (IVF), compared with 956 live births in 1988.[2] Midwives should have an understanding of the legal issues involved and the framework which has been established. The major scientific developments which are taking place in the fields of genetic engineering, genetic screening and genetic selection raise many ethical and legal issues with which the midwife should be conversant so that she can provide the professional support and understanding which her clients are entitled to expect.

The present law dates from the Warnock report which was published in 1984.[3] Many of its recommendations were subsequently incorporated into the Human Fertilization and Embryology Act 1990, which covers the topics shown in Table 1.

Human Fertilization and Embryology Authority (HFEA)

This authority is appointed by the Secretary of State for Health as a statutory non-Crown body. The Secretary of State also appoints

- The chairman and deputy chairman. (Anyone involved with commissioning or funding research is ineligible.)
- Registered medical practitioners.
- Those concerned with keeping or using gametes (sperm and ova) or embryos outside the body.

The functions of the HFEA are shown in Table 2.

Table 1. Human Fertilization and Embryology Act 1990

- Establishes a statutory authority, the HFEA
- Prohibits specific activities in connection with embryos and gametes
- Enables licences to be issued by the HFEA
- Defines 'mother' and 'father'
- Regulates disclosure of information and confidentiality
- Provides a defence of a conscientious objection
- Gives powers of enforcement and creates offences
- Makes provision in relation to the giving and withdrawal of consent

Table 2. Functions of the Human Fertilization and Embryology Authority

- Keep under review information about embryos and advise the Secretary of State
- Publicize the services provided to the public by the Authority
- Provide advice and information for persons to whom licences apply or who are receiving treatment
- Grant, vary, suspend and revoke licences through licence committees
- Issue directions either generally or specifically
- Maintain a code of practice giving guidance about the conduct of activities and treatment services
- Maintain a register containing specified information.

The Act regulates activities in respect of embryos (either a live human embryo where fertilization is complete or an ovum in the process of fertilization) outside the human body and gametes (unfertilized ova or sperm). The activities shown in Table 3 and 4 are prohibited.

Table 3. Prohibited activities in relation to embryos

S.3(1) No person shall:
a. Bring about the creation of an embryo, or
b. Keep or use an embryo except in pursuance of a licence.

S.3(2) No person shall place in a woman:
a. A live embryo other than a human embryo, or
b. Any live gametes other than human gametes.

S3(3) A licence cannot authorize:
a. Keeping or using an embryo after the appearance of the primitive streak (not later than the end of 14 days beginning with the day when the gametes are mixed).
b. Placing an embryo in any animal
c. Keeping or using an embryo in any circumstances in which regulations prohibit its keeping of use, or
d. Replacing a nucleus of a cell of an embryo with a nucleus taken from a cell of any person, embryo or subsequent development of an embryo.

Table 4. Prohibited activities in relation to gametes

S.4(1) No person shall:

a. Store any gametes, or
b. During treatment services, use the sperm of any man unless the services are provided for the woman and the man together or use the eggs of any other woman, or
c. Mix gametes with the live gametes of any animal, except in pursuance of a licence.

S.4(2) A licence cannot authorize storing or using gametes in any circumstances in which regulations prohibit their storage or use.

S.4(3) No person shall place sperm and eggs in a woman in any circumstances specified in the regulations except in pursuance of a licence.

The authority can grant licences authorizing:

- Activities in the course of providing treatment services
- The storage of gametes and embryos
- Activities for the purpose of a project of research

The definitions of 'mother' and 'father' for the purposes of the Act are shown in Table 5.

Table 5. Definitions of mother and father

S.27(1) The woman who is carrying or has carried a child as a result of the placing in her of an embryo or of sperm and eggs and no other woman, is to be treated as the mother of the child.

(This does not apply to adoption but applies whether the woman was in the UK or elsewhere at the time of the placing in her of an embryo or the sperm and eggs).

S.28 (1) Where a child is being or has carried by a woman as the result of the placing in her of any embryo or of sperm and eggs or her artificial insemination; if

a. At the time of placing in her of the embryo or the sperm and eggs or of her insemination, the woman was a party to a marriage, *and*
b. The creation of the embryo carried by her was not brought about with the sperm of the other party to the marriage, the other party to the marriage shall be treated as the father of the child unless it is shown that he did not consent to the placing in her of the embryo or the sperm and eggs or to her insemination.

If the treatment services were provided for her and a man together by a person to whom a licence applies, then he shall be treated as the father of the child.

> Where the sperm of a man is given for the treatment of others under paragraph 5 of schedule 3 or the sperm of a man or any embryo created from his sperm is used after his death, he is not treated as the father of the child.
>
> Under section 30 the courts can make orders providing for a child to be treated in law as the child of the parties to the marriage in certain circumstances.

Disclosure of information and confidentiality

Section 33 prohibits any member or employee of a licensing authority disclosing information which is contained in the register so that an individual can be identified. However the consent of the person(s) protected by these confidentiality provisions can release the person from the prohibition. The Human Fertilization and Embryology (Disclosure of Information) Act 1992 was passed to enable additional exceptions to the duty of confidentiality to be recognized.

The bar on a doctor passing information direct to the patient's GP has been lifted. The 1992 Act enables the patient to give consent to disclosure to a specified person and to give general consent to disclosure within a wider circle of people where disclosure is necessary in connection with medical treatment, clinical audit or accounts audit.

Before consent is given, reasonable steps must be taken to explain the implications of giving consent to the patient. Disclosure of information is also permissible in an emergency where the person disclosing is satisfied that the disclosure is necessary to avert imminent danger to the health of the patient and at the time it is not reasonably practicable to obtain the patient's consent.

The clinician can also disclose information to his legal adviser where necessary for the purposes preliminary to or in connection with legal proceedings. The 1992 Act allows access to records of treatment to be given to personal representatives and those bringing litigation on behalf of the incapacitated patient. Power is given for new regulations relating to additional exceptions to the principle of confidentiality to be made if necessary.

Disclosure in the interests of justice

These can be made under section 34 in proceedings before a court when the question of whether a person is or is not the parent of the child by virtue of the Act fails to be determined.

Disclosure in relation to Congenital Disabilities (Civil Liability) Act 1976

The court can make an application to the HFEA authorizing it to disclose information kept in the register and relevant to the issue of parentage.

Enforcement provisions and offences

The powers of enforcement given to the HFEA and its members and employees are considerable, and include:

On entering and inspecting premises, the right to:

- Take possession of anything which he has reasonable grounds to believe may be required.
- Take steps to preserve anything or prevent interference with anything. If there are reasonable suspicions that an

offence has occurred a warrant can be obtained from a Justice of the Peace to enter premises, using such forces as is necessary, and to search premises.

Offences include:

- Undertaking activities prohibited by section 3(2) or 4(1)(c) without a licence or doing anything which cannot be authorized by a licence.

- Providing false or misleading information for the purposes of a licence.

- Disclosing information in contravention of the Act.

The consent of the Director of Public Prosecutions is required before proceedings can be commenced.

Consent to treatment

The 1990 Act makes very detailed provisions relating to the giving and use of gametes and embryos and the Act requires counselling to be given before consent is obtained.

Schedule 3 covers the consent to the use of gametes or embryos. Consent has to be given in writing and effective consent means consent which has not been withdrawn. The provisions of the schedule are set out in Table 6.

Use of gametes for the treatment of others

A person's gametes must not be used for the purposes of treatment services unless there is an effective consent by that person to their being so used and they are in accordance with the terms of the consent. A person's gametes must not be received for use for those purposes unless there is an effective consent by that person to their being so used. This paragraph does not apply to the use of a person's gametes for that person, or that person and another together, receiving treatment services.

IVF and subsequent use of embryos

A person's gametes must not be used to bring about creation of any embryo *in vitro* unless there is an effective consent by that person to any embryo, the creation of which may be brought about with the use of those gametes, being used for one or more of the purposes mentioned by the Table 6. Each person whose gametes were used for IVF must give an effective consent before the embryo can be received.

Table 6. Consent provisions
Consent to the use of an embryo must specify one or more of the following uses: • Providing treatment services to the person giving consent, or that person and another specified person together • Providing treatment services to persons not including the person giving the consent, or • For the purposes of any project of research, and may specify conditions subject to which the embryo may be so used.
A consent to the storage of any gametes or embryos must: • Specify the maximum period of storage (if less than the statutory storage period), and • State what is to be done with the gametes or embryo if the person who gave the consent dies or is unable because of incapacity to vary the terms of the consent or to revoke it, and may specify conditions subject to which the gametes or embryo may remain in storage.
Other matters to be included in the consent can be specified by the HFEA.

> Before a person gives consent under this Schedule, she or he must be:
>
> - Given a suitable opportunity to receive proper counselling about the implications of taking proposed steps, and
> - Provided with such relevant information as is proper.
> - Informed of his/her right to withdraw consent or vary it at any time by notice given by the person who gave the consent to the person keeping the gametes or embryo to which the consent is relevant.
>
> However, the terms of any consent to the use of any embryo cannot be varied, and such consent cannot be withdrawn, once the embryo has been used:
>
> - In providing treatment services, or
> - For the purposes of any project of research.

Embryos obtained by lavage

An embryo taken from a woman must not be used for any purpose unless there is an effective consent by her to the use of the embryo for that purpose and it is used in accordance with that consent.

Storage of gametes and embryos

There must be an effective consent by the person whose gametes are to be stored and storage must be in accordance with their consent.

References

1. HFEA (1994). *Annual Report.* London: HFEA.
2. *ILA Statistical Analysis of UK IVF Data 1985-90* (available from HFEA, 30 Artillery Lane, London, E1 7LS. Tel: 0171 377 5077).
3. (1984) *Report of the Committee of Inquiry into Fertilization and Embryology.* (Warnock report). London: HMSO.

Reproduced with kind permission from Modern Midwife, December, 1994

The Scope of Fertility Treatment

Bridgit Dimond continues her review of the law relating to fertilization

Last month, we considered the provisions of the Human Fertilization and Embryology Act 1990, including the establishment of the Human Fertilization and Embryology Authority (HFEA).

The HFEA has published a Code of Practice[1] which its 67 licensed centres must observe. This includes the decisions over who can obtain *in vitro fertilization* (IVF) treatment.

Media interest has recently focused on fertility treatment offered to post-menopausal women. Last year it was reported that a 62-year old woman gave birth after IVF treatment by Dr Severino Antinori in Italy.[2] The baby was conceived from the sperm of the husband and a donated egg and delivered by caesarean section. The couple's 17 year-old son had died in a motor accident three years before the treatment.

It is unlikely that any licensed centre in the United Kingdom following the Code of Practice would approve the donation of eggs in such circumstances, although the HFEA has set no age limit.

Similarly, the implantation of an embryo in a man, as reported in 1991, causes concern and could not be undertaken under HFEA guidelines. Doctors in Johannesburg announced the delivery, by laparotomy, of the first baby (a 9lb 6oz girl) born to a human male. A fertilized egg was implanted within the man's abdominal cavity where it attached to the abdominal wall, developed a placenta and grew to maturity.[3] Sperm and ova were taken from the couple. The wife, who had a five year old child, could not have a second baby safely. The man received female hormone injections throughout the pregnancy and went for regular antenatal checks.

There is no enforceable statutory right for a person to be given IVF treatment and the Code of Practice advises the licensed centres on which people to treat. There is a statutory duty to 'take account of the welfare of any child who may be born as a result of the treatment (including the need of that child for a father), and of any other child who may be affected by the birth'[4] before a woman is offered treatment. Of 45, 000 women offered IVF treatment between August 1991 and July 1994, 25 have been over 50 years and five of these have given birth.[5]

Currently, fewer than 25 per cent of women conceive and give birth following IVF treatment. A midwife may be involved in providing considerable support for clients undergoing such therapy. As progress is made in the field of assisted reproduction, treatment may be more widely available, in which case there may be increasing pressure from infertile couples demanding IVF facilities within the NHS. Midwives might become more involved in the care of mothers undergoing IVF treatment and in protecting the couples' privacy.

Use of ovarian tissue

Public concern was raised in 1993 when it was reported that cells from expelled fetuses were being used in the course of IVF.[4] There is a shortage of donated eggs and the use of tissue collected from such sources could go far in meeting the shortage.

Responding to public opinion generated by this document, the HFEA banned the use of ovaries taken from aborted fetuses to treat childless women,[5] and also banned the use of donor ovaries from cadavers in treatment, on the grounds that further consideration was required of the issues. However, the authority was prepared to permit research to be carried out on fetal ovaries as well as those taken from cadavers and live donors.

The wrong embryos

If licensed centres fail to follow the HFEA Code of Practice they could lose their licence. It was recently reported that two mothers undergoing IVF had been mistakenly implanted with embryos belonging to other couples. This should be impossible if the recommended procedures are closely followed and monitored. The HFEA was quick to point out that in one case, no pregnancy resulted, and in the other, the mistake was realized immediately. The HFEA acts as a watchdog to ensure that action is taken to ensure such errors are not repeated.

References

1. HFEA (1993). *Code of Practice.* London: HFEA.
2. *The Times* (1994). 19th July.
3. *Health Alert* (1991). 7(123). p.331.
4. HFEA (1994). *Donated Ovarian Tissue in Embryo Research and Assisted Conception.* (Public Consultation Document). London: HFEA.
5. HFEA (1994). *Donated Ovarian Tissue in Embryo Research and Assisted Conception.* (Report). London: HFEA.

Reproduced with kind permission from Modern Midwife, January, 1995

Index

A

abortion 38
access 30
  to records 32
acting without consent 26
Acts of Parliament 2
  Abortion Act (1967) 12, 88
  Children Act (1989) 88
  Congenital Disabilities (Civil Liability) Act (1976) 86
  Congenital Disabilities Act (1976) 84, 85
  Consumer Protection Act (1987) 50, 85
  Health and Safety Act (1974) 50
  Human Fertilization and Embryology Act (1990) 12, 84, 86
  Medicines Act (1968) 76
  Nurses, Midwives and Health Visitors Act (1979) 3, 6
  Occupier's Liability Act (1957) 4, 50
  Road Traffic Act 11
  Suicide Act (1961) 6
  Trade Union and Labour Relations Act (1993) 45
administration of medicines
  UKCC guidance 77
AIDS 52
antenatal 33
APEL 1, 12, 14, 64
assault 6
assessment opportunity 73
audit 23

B

babies 26
barristers 2
benefit 25

birth at home 37, 65
birth plans 23, 25
Bolam Test 5, 26, 38
brain damaged 37
breach of confidentiality 31
  of contract 6
  of duty 60
  of contract of employment 45
  of the duty of care 27, 37, 39
  of trust 30
burden of proof 10

C

caesarean section 26
causation 37, 61
Changing Childbirth 23, 33, 34, 56, 65, 66, 73
Children Act (1989) 88
civil liability 10, 37
client centred care 23
client held records 33
Clothier report 16
Code of Professional Conduct (1992) 6, 15, 50
Codes of Practice 20
collaborative care planning 34
collective bargaining 45
common law 2, 4, 11
communication 23
community care 56
community midwifery 65, 70
compensation 37, 41
competence 20
complaints 30
  policy 34
computer stored data 34
computers 34
conditions of service 43
confidentiality 12, 30
Congenital Disabilities (Civil Liability) Act (1976) 86
Congenital Disabilities Act (1976) 84, 85
conscientious objection 12
consent 12
  to treatment 23, 26

135

Consumer Protection Act (1987) 50, 85
consumer representatives 24
contract law 44
contract of employment 43
contractual duty 56
coroners 7
court
    different types of 6
    evidence in 33
    functions of 6
    reports 5
    hearing 39
credit 92
criminal offence 30
criminal proceedings 30
critical incident 18
cultural needs 27

D

dangerous substances 53
dangers at work 53
death 7
    registered 7
decisions 23
defences 25, 39
demand 24
directive 3
disciplinary proceedings 11
disclosure 31
drug addict 32, 79
duty of care 37
    breach of 27
duty to give information 23

E

employer/employee
    relationship of 43
employment law 7, 43, 57
ethics 2
ethnic 27
European community 51
    law 2
European laws 3
evidence-based care 24

F

fetal monitoring 38
fetus
    status and rights 84
fertility treatment 133

G

government 43
GP fundholders 70
GPs 67
Guidelines to Professional Practice
    (1996) 30, 76

H

harm 25, 37
health and safety
    committees 57
    in the community 71
    in the future 62
    law 50
        basic principles 50
    representatives 57
health authority 16
hepatitis 53
HIV positive 32, 52
home birth 65

I

independent midwives 43, 47, 55
indicators of success 23
industrial action 45, 46
industrial tribunal 7, 34
infectious diseases 52
information giving 23
Informed Choice 24
injunction 30
inquest 34
insurance cover 57
interviewing 15
IVF 32, 128

J

job description 44
judges 2

L

labour 38
law 2
  common 4
  civil 6
  criminal 6
  distinction from ethics 11
  and in vitro fertilization 125
  specific areas 82
legal language 11
legal personnel 2, 9
legal system 1
legal terms 11
legislative framework 76
liability 56
limitation of time 39
litigation 39
local bargaining 43, 44
local pay guidance 114
local standards 38
local supervising authority (LSA) 4, 16, 55

M

managers 40
manual handling 51
Maternity Services Liaison Committee (MSLC) 66
medical examination 4
medical records 34
medication
  administering and prescribing 78, 125
  and the midwife 121
  legal aspects of 76
MIDIRS 24
midwife managed units 65, 71, 116
midwifery led unit 69
midwifery practice 16

Midwife's Code of Practice (1994) 6, 15, 50
midwives 16
  and complementary therapy 38, 109
Midwives Rules (1993) 2, 3, 6, 15, 20
misconduct 19
module 18
mother 25
  views of 26
multi-disciplinary team 31

N

national security 31
needs 24
negligence 10, 27, 37, 39
NHS
  Centre for Reviews and Dissemination 24
  Management Executive 53
  trusts 40

O

obstetric care 39
Organizational Standards for Maternity Services (1995) 66

P

PCC hearing 19
personal injury 37, 56
personal professional profile *vii, ix*
plaintiff 50
Post Registration Education and Practice (PREP) 20
postnatal care 23
practice developments 18
practice nurse 68
preceptor *x*
  preparing to be a 91
pregnancy 23
prenatal screening 40

procedures 38
  civil 10
  court hearing 39
  criminal proceedings 9
professional accountability 15
professional conduct committee 11
professional conduct proceedings 18
professional misconduct 11, 106
professional organization 10
professional standards 25
prosecutor 50
protocols 16, 38
psychiatric illness 32
public interest 31

Q

quantum 41, 61

R

race discrimination 47
record keeping 39
  and medicines 79
  standards 33
records 11, 30
redundancy 44
refresher study days 20
regulation 3
risk management 40
Royal College of General Practitioners 65
Royal College of Midwives 10, 45, 51, 65
Royal College of Nursing 10

S

Scope of Professional Practice (1992) 77
selection of staff 15
self review 20
sex discrimination 47
sexually transmitted disease 32
shirodkar suture 37

significant incident 18
situations of necessity 26
solicitors 2
sources of law
  common 2
  statute 2, 11
special situations 40
Standards for the Administration of Medicines (1992) 77
standards of care 38
statute law 2, 11
statutory instruments 3
  interpretation of 3
statutory provisions
  in childbirth and death 82
statutory rights 44, 47
statutory supervision 17
still birth 83
stress at work 58
strike 45
  action 45
supervision 16
supervisors of midwives 8, 16
surrogate 32
suspended from practice 4

T

targets 23
termination 12
tort 6, 37
Trade Union and Labour Relations Act (1993) 45
trade union representative 8
translation 27
trespass 23, 24
  to the person 27
trespassers 4

U

UKCC 13
  Code of Professional Conduct (1992) 6, 15, 50
  Guidelines to Professional Practice (1996) 30, 76

Midwife's Code of Practice (1994) 6, 15, 50
Scope of Professional Practice (1992) 77
Standards for the Administration of Medicines (1992) 77
Standards for Records and Record Keeping (1993) 33
Codes 2, 6
ultrasound 27
unbiased information 26
unfair dismissal 7, 46
unlawful 46
untoward incidents 40

V

valid consent 27
valid refusal 26
vicarious liability 10
victimization 57
violence 53
Vitamin K 27

W

wants 24
Welsh Health Planning Forum 69
whistle blowing 13, 57
Wilson report 34, 69
'working to grade' 45